Father Brown Reforms the Liturgy

FATHER BROWN
Reforms the Liturgy

BEING THE TRACT
Why Revive the Liturgy, and How?

Monsignor
JOHN O'CONNOR,
CHESTERTON'S "FATHER BROWN"

As introduced, edited & annotated by
HUGH SOMERVILLE KNAPMAN OSB

AROUCA
PRESS

In association with
The Weldon Press, Woolhampton

Cum permissu superiorum

ISBN: 978-1-989905-38-8 (pbk)
ISBN: 978-1-989905-39-5 (hardcover)

Arouca Press
PO Box 55003
Bridgeport PO
Waterloo, ON N2J3G0
Canada
www.aroucapress.com
Send inquiries to info@aroucapress.com

Book and cover design by
Michael Schrauzer

The caricature of Father Brown is gratefully
used with the permission of the artist.

For
Mother Church

CONTENTS

ACKNOWLEDGMENTS

While the editor's failings herein are entirely his own, any merits attaching to the introduction which precedes or the notes which follow will be in no small measure due to the help received from: Abbess Anna Brennan, Dame Laurentia Johns, Dame Philippa Edwards, and the Community of Stanbrook Abbey; Dame Margaret Truran of Monastero di Santa Cecilia in Trastevere, Rome; Ms Carol Langham, Archivist at the Chartered Association of Building Engineers; Mr Robert Finnigan, the Archivist of the Diocese of Leeds; Mr Scott Jacobs of the Williams Andrews Clark Memorial Library at the University of California, Los Angeles; Mr Noel McFerran and Ms Sarah Stiller at the John M. Kelly Library at Saint Michael's College, University of Toronto; Ms Clare Halliday, administrator at Our Lady and the First Martyrs of Rome in Bradford; Monsignor Andrew Burnham; Dr Brian Sudlow of Aston University; Dr Andrew Cichy of Perth, Western Australia; Abbot Geoffrey Scott, Archivist of Douai Abbey; Father Gervase Holdaway of Douai Abbey; and others whom my memory in its frailty fails now to recall by name.

CAVEAT LECTOR

While the initial research for this book began late in 2019, it was soon interrupted by the global crisis attending Covid-19, and the travel restrictions this imposed. Thus, the majority of the research has been conducted using books at hand, and the extensive, though neither infallible nor inexhaustible, resources of the internet. Any resulting lacunae in this pandemic production will be addressed in a possible future edition.

Ut in omnibus glorificetur Deus.

INTRODUCTION

In the library at Douai Abbey a slim tract, housed in a recycled envelope, lies largely undisturbed and unrecognised among the scores of more substantial volumes on the liturgy shelves. The envelope bears a title and shelf mark, but for the authorship and publication date there is only a question mark. On reading, the tract arouses deeper interest beyond this initial mystery, fed by the tract's apparent age, the text that concludes the tract declaring that it is "For private circulation only," and for its self-confident title: *Why Revive the Liturgy, and How?* (hereafter, *Liturgy*). A little research has settled some of the mystery.

AUTHORSHIP

The tract's authorship is easily determined. A copy of *Liturgy* can be found in the library of the University of Toronto. It nestles among the Monsignor John O'Connor Papers held there, which are part of the Chesterton Collection donated by Father Kevin Scannell.[1] On the title page Father Scannell (presumably) has written:

> This pamphlet was written by Fr. John O'Connor (Chesterton's Father Brown) when as parish priest of St. Cuthberts [sic] Bradford, he was planning a new church to be built on Hights lane [sic]. The architect, Jack Langtry-Langton was a young man of the parish who was young enough to

---

1 Father (later Monsignor) Kevin Scannell (1902–1976) was a priest of the diocese of Leeds. Four of his brothers were also priests. He was a dedicated collector of Chestertonia. His collection was donated in 1969 to the Pontifical Institute of Medieval Studies in Toronto, prompted by Father Scannell's dismay that "no one in Britain seems to appreciate that Chesterton was a great theological and philosophical writer and a brilliant thinker. It is different on the other side of the Atlantic." (*Catholic Herald* [22 August 1969]: 2).

do what he was told by his P. P. The Church, dedicated to Our Lady of the First Martyrs [sic] was built in 1935.[2]

His information on the dating of the tract will be of further interest below, as will the church of Our Lady and the First Martyrs.

Another reference to *Liturgy* can be found in an article entitled "The Prescience of Father Brown," in *The Clergy Review* of February 1972, by Dame Felicitas Corrigan, a Benedictine nun of Stanbrook Abbey. In it she describes her own happenchance discovery of the tract, while sorting through "a mountain of pamphlets acquired during seventy years of monastic life by our late Abbess, Dame Laurentia McLachlan."[3] Most of the pamphlets Dame Felicitas found passé and fit for the bonfire. However, among them she spotted a copy of *Liturgy*, "stitched in one gathering of thirty-four leaves between khaki hammered paper wrappers." From it slipped a covering letter from Monsignor O'Connor to Abbess Laurentia, dated 9 August 1939. Of the tract it accompanied he writes revealingly:

> What jobation could be made on the enclosed if I were with you! Worse than Barney Shaw [ie George Bernard Shaw] shaking the bars of your cage! And how lacking is the tract in classical restraint and in logical order! It might then be as boring as most of our careful writers, and no one would get through it. If you want to

---

2 A transcription can be found at https://search.library.utoronto.ca/details?632396.

3 Margaret Laurentia McLachlan (1866–1953) was clothed in the English Benedictine habit at Stanbrook Abbey in 1884, and was elected its abbess in 1931. She was much devoted to the restoration of Gregorian chant. Her friendship with the playwright George Bernard Shaw and the antiquarian Sir Sydney Cockerell was dramatized in Hugh Whitemore's play, *The Best of Friends*.

scandalize any Pious Person by lending him this, you may have another copy or even several. I put you in the Mass for tomorrow hoping that blood pressure will remit sufficiently to let you take my reflections lying down at least.

As Dame Felicitas herself concludes, "So the mystery of authorship was solved."[4] This letter, too, will be of interest regarding the date of *Liturgy*'s publication.

A third and fleeting reference to *Liturgy* as O'Connor's is found in his 2010 biography by Julia Smith. Smith states that the tract was "probably written about 1928"[5] but she gives no basis for this assertion, though some are in agreement.[6] Yet, presumably on the authority of Father Scannell's note, others have accepted 1935 as its publication date.[7] Neither dating will bear close scrutiny.

John O'Connor (1870–1952) was a pupil at the small school run by the English Benedictines at the priory of Saint Edmund in Douai, France (now at Douai Abbey in Berkshire, though its school closed in 1999). A native of County Tipperary, his initial education with the Franciscans was unhappy, but after a couple of happier years under the Christian Brothers he was sent to the English monks in France, where he flourished as a school-boy and thereafter remained a faithful old-boy. On leaving Douai he studied at the English College in Rome, gaining a Licentiate in Sacred Theology, and was ordained on 30 March 1895 by Archbishop the Hon. Edmund Stonor in the basilica of Saint John Lateran in Rome, for the diocese of Leeds in Yorkshire.

---

4   D. Felicitas Corrigan, "The Prescience of Father Brown," *The Clergy Review* (February 1972): 84.

5   Julia Smith, *The Elusive Father Brown: The Life of Mgr John O'Connor* (Leominster: Gracewing, 2010), 146.

6   e.g., Judith Collins, *Eric Gill: The Sculpture* (New York: Overlook Press, 1998), 42.

7   e.g., Richard Giles, *Re-pitching the Tent: Re-ordering the Church Building for Worship and Mission* (Collegeville, MN: The Liturgical Press, 1999), 250.

Father O'Connor passed his entire priestly life serving parishes in Yorkshire's West Riding. He was a man of considerable gifts and varied interests, with a wide acquaintance that went beyond Catholic circles. One of his earlier non-Catholic friends was G. K. Chesterton (1874–1936), esteemed to this day as an insightful Catholic writer and formidable apologist. O'Connor first made contact with Chesterton by letter in February 1903, while serving as a curate in Keighley. The friendship was undoubtedly crucial to Chesterton's eventual conversion to Catholicism some two decades later. Among Chesterton's most popular works are his "Father Brown" detective stories, 53 in all, published between 1910 and 1936, still in print and adapted more than once for both the large and small screens. Though the likeness is not exact, nor was it intended to be, Father Brown was acknowledged to have been inspired by Father O'Connor. O'Connor was not backward in trading on this association with Chesterton's detecting cleric, authoring books and articles identifying with his fictional *alter ego*.

O'Connor received Chesterton into the Church on 30 July 1922, at the Railway Hotel in Beaconsfield, with their mutual friend, Father Ignatius Rice OSB (1883–1955), a monk of Douai Abbey, as witness. Chesterton's wife Frances followed him into the Church four years later.

One notable characteristic of Father (from 1937, Monsignor) O'Connor was the uncommon conjunction in his person of a lifelong parish priest with a man of developed literary, artistic and intellectual tastes, and blessed with a continental education. His tastes could find strong expression, as his parish choir would discover. An accomplished writer and raconteur, he was *au fait* with both Church and society. It is his standing as a professional pastor widely read in theology and culture that lends his *Liturgy* an added interest.

DATE OF PUBLICATION

Liturgy was printed privately and anonymously. The copies bear no date, nor any mention of a printer or publisher. It may have been printed in Bradford where O'Connor had other works printed, such as his volume of sermons, *A Month of Sundays: The Foolishness of Father Brown*, from the presses of Lonsdale and Bartholomew in an undated volume which Smith dates to 1940. It is hardly surprising that no record has been found of how many copies of the tract were printed or to whom they were sent.

If, as Smith asserts in O'Connor's biography, *Liturgy* was published in 1928, then it is inconceivable that O'Connor's old friend Chesterton, a spiritual son with whom he was in regular and close contact, would not have received a copy. Yet, on searching the Chesterton papers held both in North America and the British Library, no reference to *Liturgy* could be found. His correspondence with O'Connor, and with the Douai monk Father Ignatius Rice, likewise show no trace of it. Could O'Connor have excluded them from the tract's distribution, perhaps out of tact; or did these two close friends of his maintain an *omertà* more resolute than O'Connor himself was able to maintain, if his letter to Abbess Laurentia is any evidence? Either possibility is unsatisfactory. Another should be considered: perhaps *Liturgy* was not published in 1928 or 1935, but later.

At the beginning of *Liturgy* O'Connor contends that for "nearly sixty years the Liturgy has been more dear to me than eyesight, space or liberty." Since he was born on 5 December 1870, dating the tract to 1928 would find him aged 58, which is indeed "nearly sixty." However, it is unlikely that he was devoted to the liturgy from birth. Smith records that O'Connor "first realized his existence" when he was about 18 months old.[8] He began his education, a "miserable and

---

8   Smith, *The Elusive Father Brown*, 6.

degrading waste of time,"[9] with the Franciscans in Clonmel, Ireland at Easter 1877, when he was six years of age. After the friars' school closed four years later, he spent two academically-successful years with the Christian Brothers before being sent abroad to Douai.

O'Connor had a vastly happier time at the school of the English Benedictines at Saint Edmund's Priory in Douai, French Flanders, where he found "the monks were our big brothers and we had a sort of feeling of going shares with them in everything."[10] It was here, aged 16, that he first became "God-conscious."[11] Of course, his love of the liturgy may well have pre-dated that deepening of faith.

He arrived at Douai School on Assumption Day in 1883, when he was aged 12. He found in the monastic Vespers something to bring his soul close to "ecstasy."[12] It is notable that in *Liturgy* he excludes the Divine Office, of which Vespers is a part, from his programme for liturgical reform. It is not unreasonable to suspect that his love of the Mass had begun before his arrival at Douai in 1883. Unfamiliar with Vespers, he would have been familiar enough with the Mass, and almost certainly he was an experienced altar server. If "nearly sixty years" were dated from his time with the Christian Brothers, this would suggest that the publication of *Liturgy* was in the late 1930s.

In *Liturgy* O'Connor refers to "Spain before the cataclysm," almost certainly a reference to the Spanish Civil War of 1936–39. It is true that Spain was in turmoil for some years before the civil war, and the period after November 1933, when a right-wing government was formed in Spain, was indeed known as "the black two years" by many. Nevertheless,

---

9   Ibid.
10   John O'Connor, "Old Douai," *The Douai Magazine* 15, no. 1 (Spring 1948), 10.
11   Smith, *The Elusive Father Brown*, 9.
12   Ibid., 10.

it is doubtful that these pre-civil war years could justify the label "cataclysm."

Father Scannell's note on his copy of *Liturgy* is more ambiguous, and implies rather than asserts 1935 as the year of its production. He claims that *Liturgy* was written by O'Connor while, as parish priest of Saint Cuthbert's in Bradford (1919–1952), he was planning to build a chapel of ease in Heights Lane — Our Lady and the First Martyrs — which "was built in 1935." This church certainly embodies many of the principles advanced in *Liturgy*. The building's foundation stone was laid in 1934 and the church opened in 1935.

Smith's biography of O'Connor is vague as to when he first began actively planning for the church in Heights Lane. However, in the brief history of the parish that introduces the order of service for the church's consecration on 19 March 1974, George Bradley writes that,

> By the end of the twenties Fr. O'Connor decided on the necessity of building a new church to serve this part of his parish.[13]

So, if the monograph was written while O'Connor was planning the church as Father Scannell confidently asserts, this could date *Liturgy* to a period from the late 1920s to 1934. This offers some justification for Smith's dating of *Liturgy* to 1928 while not ruling out a dating up to even 1935, though both years are at best circumstantial. After all, Father Scannell mentions 1935 only as the year in which the church was built.

Here Dame Felicitas Corrigan's article cited above becomes particularly relevant. She quotes O'Connor's excited covering letter of 9 August 1939 to the abbess that accompanied her copy of *Liturgy*. Clearly O'Connor appreciates, and apparently

---

13   George Bradley, "A Brief History of the Parish of First Martyrs," in *Consecration Ceremony of the Church of Our Lady and the First Martyrs* (Bradford, 1974), 9.

intends, that *Liturgy* would constitute something of an ecclesiastical hand-grenade. The tract's decidedly indiscreet manner of expression was something he took no pains to mitigate. Here, by the by, would be ample motive to keep *Liturgy* free of any indication of authorship, date, or place of printing. O'Connor would not have been so gauche as to embarrass his bishop, and he would equally have wanted to avoid giving his bishop a stick with which to beat him, or sufficient cause to commit him to Bedlam.

More significant is the date of this letter. If written in 1928, or even 1935, then *Liturgy* would surely not have been as fresh in 1939 as O'Connor's letter to Abbess Laurentia strongly implies. Why get so excited about something written five or eleven years earlier? As a friend and regular correspondent of Abbess Laurentia, O'Connor delaying so many years in sending her his tract makes as little sense as not sending it to Chesterton.

A letter from O'Connor to another nun-friend at Stanbrook, Dame Werburg Welch,[14] is noteworthy. Written seven months later, on 4 March 1940, O'Connor tells her:

> If Lady Abbess is in ruder health, tell her my "Liturgy" has been read in the Refectory of a House of Studies!

Given his letter the previous August to Abbess Laurentia, what else could this "Liturgy" be but the tract? If it had been written in 1928 or 1935, it seems strange for it to appear years later in a conventual refectory[15] when it would have

---

14 Eileen Werburg Welch (1894–1990) was clothed in the English Benedictine habit at Stanbrook Abbey in 1915. She studied art under the Ditchling figures Eric Gill and Desmond Chute. Her brother, Oliver, was a master in the school at Douai Abbey. The 1955 Stations of the Cross in Douai's abbey church were carved by the Douai monk Dom Aloysius Bloor to Dame Werburg's design.

15 No further clue has been found to identify the adventurous house of studies, but given O'Connor's long-standing links with the forward-thinking

been growing dimmer even in its author's memory. The clear impression from this second letter, too, is that *Liturgy* is so topical because so recent.

Incidentally, since it is clear that O'Connor posted a copy of *Liturgy* to Abbess Laurentia, it seems safe to assume that the celebrated Stanbrook Abbey Press did not print *Liturgy*, an assumption reinforced by the relatively poor quality of its production, inferior to the fine printing for which the nuns at Stanbrook were renowned.

What, then, of Father Scannell's covering note which dates the tract to the period in which the church of Our Lady and First Martyrs was first conceived and built (1928–35)? His apparent dating comes up against the nigh-insuperable obstacle of Chesterton's absolute silence about *Liturgy*. Chesterton died in 1936, and it is inconceivable that he would not have been sent a copy of *Liturgy* given his close relationship with O'Connor.

Scannell's note on the title-page of his copy could be read as implying that *Liturgy* served as a manifesto guiding the design of First Martyrs in Bradford by the young and biddable architect, Jack Langtry-Langton. The Langtry-Langton firm is still operating in Bradford but, alas, did not respond to my enquiries. However, Jack Langtry-Langton refers in his notes for the consecration of the church in 1974 to "Fr O'Connor's original planning brief"[16] for the design of the church, which Langtry-Langton had to adapt to meet the demands of cost and geography. It would be interesting to see this original brief in full.

Some idea of it emerges in Langtry-Langton's reminiscence which concludes the booklet produced for the consecration

---

Dominicans, either of their contemporary houses of formation, Blackfriars in Oxford or Hawkesyard in Staffordshire, would rank high on the list of suspects.

16 Jack Langtry-Langton, "The Architect Remembers" in *Consecration Ceremony*, 30.

of First Martyrs in 1974. He reveals that the church was not built to the original design, which had been

> based upon a Greek cross, surmounted by an octagonal clerestory or drum, surmounted by a semi-circular dome. The domed building would have been an impressive sight on Heights Lane, and the whole design pleased Father O'Connor, for his basic requirements of the centrally placed altar had been fulfilled, and by means of careful placing of the eight columns and arches supporting the clerestory, every member of the congregation had an uninterrupted view of the Sanctuary.[17]

However, the difficulties of building on a sloping site "to Father O'Connor's brief, as the central altar placing demanded a broad building,"[18] and the architect's misjudgement in including every cost in the tender, made the project too expensive in the view of the diocese. Though O'Connor "nearly lost all interest," Langtry-Langton submitted a new design which won acceptance. This proposed a round church, encompassing elements we can identify as part of O'Connor's brief, including the requirement that the church "could be used during the week for a Parochial Hall" which entailed that the altar and its rails, as well as the congregational seating, were able to be removed to the basement. The altar could be moved without disturbing the tabernacle because "Father O'Connor had asked for it [the tabernacle] to be placed on a permanent altar of repose, in the centre recess arch . . ."[19]

The architect's son, Peter (also an architect), gives further evidence of O'Connor's brief in his reflection on the occasion of the church's golden jubilee in 1985:

---

17 Ibid.
18 Ibid.
19 Ibid., 32.

> His brief to my father was clear: To make a build-
> ing in which the liturgy of the word, and the
> eucharist [sic], would be clear and understandable,
> and in intimate contact with the people.[20]

The consonance between the church and the tract is clear. What is curious is O'Connor's apparent loss of interest after the original plan was vetoed. *Liturgy* exhibits anything but a lack of interest in the setting of worship. Indeed, it is bubbling with outspoken excitement, matching that which O'Connor manifests in his letters to the nuns at Stanbrook. Perhaps it is an excitement fuelled by the successful completion of the church in Heights Lane in line with at least some of his liturgical principles. It all rather suggests a date after 1935.

One final piece of evidence needs consideration before settling on a dating. Another of O'Connor's wide acquaintance, the sculptor, carver and typographer Eric Gill, had a copy of *Liturgy* in 1938, though it seems it was on loan as he returned it after having copied it out.[21] Gill did more than merely read it; he promoted and enacted many of its principles while respecting O'Connor's anonymity. More on that will follow below. The crucial thing here is that in 1938 Gill was able to read O'Connor's tract, but apparently not able to keep it. This strongly suggests he was given access to a draft of *Liturgy*.

Therefore, it is increasingly tenable, in the absence of any justification for either published dating of the tract, that both Julia Smith and Father Scannell have ventured a guess and missed the mark, and that dating publication to after 14 June 1936 (Chesterton's death), and more specifically to

---

20   Peter Langtry-Langton, "The Architecture of the Round Church", in *1935–1985 Golden Jubilee: The Church of Our Lady and the First Martyrs* (3 June 1985): 14.

21   Eric Gill, Letter from Gill to O'Connor (6 May 1938), in *The Letters of Eric Gill*, ed. Walter Shewring (London: Jonathan Cape, 1947), #290: 403.

after 1938 (when Gill is certainly reading it, most likely in draft form) fits the evidence set out above. Such a dating would explain why no reference can be found to *Liturgy* in the papers or correspondence of G. K. Chesterton who would certainly have received a copy, and reacted to it, had he been alive when it was published. It also allows for the freshness of the tract implied in O'Connor's correspondence with the two nuns at Stanbrook in 1939–40, and its being read at a religious house of studies in early 1940.

Yet, it may be possible to reconcile to some degree all these varying guesses. It is conceivable that at the end of the 1920s, as O'Connor began to see the need for a new church in Heights Lane, he also began to reflect on the architecture and interior design of churches, and their relationship to the celebration of the Church's liturgy. It is equally conceivable that through the 1930s his opinions developed in shape and detail, and that the practicalities of building First Martyrs helped to refine further his thinking. By 1938, perhaps encouraged by the completion of his new church and the growing prominence of the Liturgical Movement, he set his reflections to paper. With a discretion that comes with age and experience, he published it anonymously, though not quite secretly, in 1939, to share with trusted friends.

In other words, though it was almost certainly born in 1939, perhaps *Liturgy* could have been a twinkle in its author's eye as early as 1928.

"LITURGY" AS A MANIFESTO

As the full title of *Liturgy* suggests, O'Connor is advocating liturgical reform while avoiding the term; he prefers to revive. Revival has less of an air of the Reformation about it. He was not alone at the time in such aspirations. The twentieth-century Liturgical Movement in the Catholic Church had found inspiration in the *motu proprio* of

Pope Saint Pius X in 1903, *Tra le sollecitudini,* on liturgical music, with its pregnant, and now rather controversial and controverted, advocacy for the "active participation" of the congregation in the celebration of the Mass. O'Connor wrote *Liturgy* when the Liturgical Movement was gathering strength on the Continent and, more slowly, in the United States and Britain. O'Connor thus may be somewhat *avant garde* among the English parochial clergy. No doubt that informs the discretion with which he published his radical tract; the first half of the twentieth century was no time for a Catholic priest to be too daring in matters of religion.

Despite the discretion of its publication, the content of *Liturgy* is bracingly indiscreet for its day, and utterly lacking "classical restraint" as O'Connor confessed to Abbess Laurentia. Safely cloaked in anonymity, he is trenchant in his opinions and their justification, which are, he admits again to the abbess, without "logical order." Some of his opinions, so breathlessly expressed, set him apart from the professional liturgical experts, not least in his often-dubious justifications of them.

For O'Connor "the liturgy" in question is the Mass alone:

> What is the Liturgy we should revive? Benediction is not the Liturgy: neither is Solemn Vespers nor Compline... The Liturgy is essentially and exclusively the solemn sacrifice of the Mass and nothing else.

He esteems the Low Mass, and while holding that from the Low Mass "must radiate the revival of the Liturgy," his exclusive focus is on "public worship," be it low Mass with a congregation or, more usually, Solemn Mass. For O'Connor, Low Mass was best fitted to non-public worship but not so suitable for public, congregational, worship, which he laments as "becoming more and more hopelessly private and peculiar."

He would preserve the Latin Canon of the Mass, "especially as I think the Latin of the Canon is our inheritance from Saint Peter himself." Nevertheless, he strongly advocates a place for the vernacular, holding that it is "merely thin rubbish to say that the use of the vernacular would obscure theological meanings. Better have them obscured than non-existent." Yet his advocacy for the vernacular is discriminating. He seeks a vernacular "specialised enough for public worship," and restricted to the congregational parts of the Mass, so that the people could take "their full and vocal share." O'Connor, like Pius X, tends to conceive of "active participation" as vocal participation. He would preserve Latin entirely "from the end of the [Mass of the] catechumens till the Communion."

O'Connor also urges a reduced eucharistic fast, and the introduction of evening Masses for the sake of the working class which a reduced fast would enable, as well as the restoration both of priestly concelebration and a permanent order of deacon. He sees no problem with the Sacred Host being received in the hand by the faithful. Many of these opinions were remarkably prescient, to be taken up in official, and unofficial, reforms beginning in the 1950s.

O'Connor's opinions on "Church Music" are confronting:

> Ah, Music! What crimes are committed in thy name!

His preference is for "the austere beauty of what I may characterise as punctuated Plain Chant," though even here he finds deleterious influences have been at work. Infamously, he once sacked his parish choir *en masse*, and while he tuts at the professionalisation of liturgical music, he still holds that "many an amateur choir should be arrested for brawling in a place of worship." He settles on a drastic solution to the problem of the music in a revived liturgy: "there shall be no music in public worship."

His overriding focus is on the nature and place of the altar, his opinions concretized in the church of Our Lady and the First Martyrs in Heights Lane. In *Liturgy* he advocates the return to a central altar as "the major reform." O'Connor desires a central altar without a tabernacle, and the congregation gathered all round it:

> The primary motive of these remarks is to burn into common consciousness that the altar must be in the middle of the place of worship, and it must be an altar and not a repository; cubic, with the table overhanging by four inches all round.

With First Martyrs he realised this aspiration. Its architect, Jack Langtry-Langton, confirms the primary consideration in the church's design: "It was built to accommodate a central altar."[22] First Martyrs was opened by Bishop Wulstan Pearson OSB on 28 May 1935, and was the first round church to be built in England in modern times. The following year First Martyrs was made a separate parish, and O'Connor had to surrender it to another priest. A parish priest was appointed in 1944 who imposed a tabernacle upon O'Connor's clean altar, adding gradines as well, both of which impeded the view of the altar from a large part of the church. No doubt these accretions would have horrified O'Connor. However, by the time the church was finally consecrated on 19 March 1974, these impositions had been undone by another priest and O'Connor's original intention honoured.

Interestingly, as early as 1915, O'Connor had built another church in the diocese, Holy Spirit in Heckmondwike. Either he had not yet formed strong liturgical opinions or lacked the courage to express them, but this church certainly has none of the radicalism of First Martyrs. Still, by adopting a "Byzantine-Romanesque" design, O'Connor seems to have

---

22   Jack Langtry-Langton, "The Church of the First Martyrs, Bradford," *The Parthenon* (March 1937): 195.

made a stand against the neo-Gothic so much in vogue. Perhaps he was inspired by the recent completion, in 1903, of the neo-Byzantine Westminster Cathedral in London.

Occasionally O'Connor wanders down more arcane liturgical byways. One such is his digression on the words *Mysterium fidei* — "the Mystery of faith" — which were part of the formula for the consecration of the chalice at Mass prior to 1969. Also of note are his eccentric forays into the history of plainchant and liturgical music, the use of unleavened bread at Mass, the colour of sacramental wine, baldacchini, saints' shrines, priestly concelebration, the style of vestments, and the reservation of the Blessed Sacrament.

However, it serves little purpose to reproduce here the detail of *Liturgy*; it is a short read and is best read in full. In it there is much to amuse, and for many there is also much to perplex, confound, annoy, and even shock. This seems to be intentional. His thinking does not fit neatly into modern categories of "progressive" or "traditionalist" which almost guarantees that *Liturgy* will poke the bears in both.

Given the continued controversy surrounding the reform of the liturgy after the Second Vatican Council, and its failure thus far to capture the hearts and minds of modern humanity as intended, and given the recent restoration of the pre-conciliar Mass as the extraordinary form of the Roman rite, O'Connor's *Liturgy* merits attention. It gives voice to what an educated, pastoral priest sought from liturgical reform before those who were entrusted with implementing the post-conciliar reform imposed on it their own agenda. At the very least, it confirms a healthy doubt about any assertion that all was liturgically paradisal before the Council.

In sum, O'Connor is exercised most particularly by three principal issues: the nature and location of the altar; the style, quality, and place of liturgical music; and the language of the Mass. His other observations and declarations generally derive from these three central concerns.

OTHER INSTANCES OF O'CONNOR'S LITURGICAL THINKING

O'Connor's priesthood was taken up with parochial work, and he was not averse to enacting his liturgical thinking in his parish ministry:

> Priests and parishioners agreed that Father O'Connor never did what was usual; being one of a kind, years ahead of his time and while not exactly a rebel, being 'antipathetic to the minutiae of the law' and not averse to bending the very rigid rules if he felt the occasion demanded it. Father Keegan recalled that almost everything brought in by the Second Vatican Council Father O'Connor had privately introduced himself years before.[23]

In a year not specified but apparently before he built First Martyrs, O'Connor preached as follows to his flock on the Fifth Sunday after Epiphany:

> Not every primitive observance is holy or indispensable, as, for instance, the offerings of bread and wine at Mass, or Communion in both kinds. The double consecration is essential to the Sacrifice but not to the Sacrament.
>
> There is an abuse a thousand years old which is to have the altar pushed to the far end of a long building, with the priest turning his back to the people. Fancy, if all representations of the Last Supper made our Lord turn His back to the Apostles.
>
> I fear we are not likely to see this reform in our time, and we are not the sort of reformers

---

23 Smith, *The Elusive Father Brown*, 70.

who burn down the house to clear it, or who
empty out the babe with the bath.

This, and other abuses stay on because men
are not only asleep, but are never perfectly awake.
Every one of us has a slack side or a blind side,
or a season of relaxation.[24]

In this example of his preaching we find the cautious
progressivism of "Father Brown" in his liturgical idealism.
While "progressive" in his opinion on the placement of the
altar and the orientation of the celebrant, he eschews any
desire to "burn down the house to clear it, or...empty out
the babe with the bath." This is an attitude he maintains
in *Liturgy*, when he adds the mitigating concession that "I
would not sweep away wholesale, but would suit my ceremonial to my circumstances. It is the paralysis of this faculty
which has led us into the mire." While he believes "not every
primitive observance is holy or indispensable," such as an
offertory procession or Communion in both the host and the
chalice, he seems to hold the ancient placement of the altar
to be as good as indispensable. While looking to ancient
practice as he believes it to be, he stops short of idolising it.

Other ancient observances which were restored, in greater
or lesser integrity, in the post-1969 liturgy are dispensable in
O'Connor's view. For example, in the homily above he does
not advocate for the offertory procession nor for Communion
in both the host and the chalice. No doubt he knows well,
and accepts, the reasons why both practices were dropped
in previous centuries. After all, the people no longer sup-
plied the bread and the wine for the Sacrifice, so it would
be artificial for them to bring up as if their own what had
been provided already by the local liturgical supplier; and
perhaps the danger of profanation and, more to O'Connor's

---

24   John O' Connor as "Father Brown", *A Month of Sundays: The Foolishness
of Father Brown* (Bradford: T. Geoghegan, no date), 34.

thinking, the demise of the ministry of the deacon, precluded regular Communion from the chalice. For O'Connor, just because something was present originally did not mean its abandonment was necessarily corruption or laxity.

Nevertheless, he could be curiously ignorant of tradition. In the same homily he offers as dubious justification for wanting the priest to face the people at the altar the apparent improbability of Jesus having turned his back to the apostles at the Last Supper. No one, in fact, would have suggested that our Lord did. However, it is not likely that he faced the apostles seated around the table as we would dine today. The accepted understanding is now that at the Last Supper Jesus and his apostles would have all sat on the same side of a low table, possibly semi-circular or U-shaped, which made for the ease of table service that formal or ceremonial meals required. The table setting in the upper room cannot helpfully be invoked to justify the celebrant's position at the altar. The Mass is not a replay of the Last Supper.

As seen above, the altar's ancient placement is an overriding concern for O'Connor. It leads to the striking "novelty" in his round church of First Martyrs of a central altar. The central altar was also important for O'Connor's liturgical fellow-traveller, Eric Gill. In his "Mass for the Masses," after setting out the socio-economic context that informs his general thinking in 1938, Gill moves to the question of the church building and its purpose, the answer to which centres on the altar:

> What is a church? There are, of course, several or many possible answers to this question, but mainly, as it seems to me, there are three: the church is (1) a preaching place, (2) a praying place, (3) a Mass house.
>
> It seems generally agreed that from a Christian and particularly the Catholic point of view the

last-named definition is the primary one. Preaching and praying take place in a church, but a church is primarily erected for the offering of the Holy Sacrifice.

The altar therefore is quite obviously the chief thing, the necessary ornament of the church, and there is no such thing as ornament except in this sense.

The altar is a place of sacrifice, on which something is offered and made holy: this is the Christian idea of a church; where there is an altar there is a church. But the circumstances of the world are such that a covering is appropriate; the climate, rain, and wind, make it necessary. And not only the altar, but the ministers, and not only the ministers, but the assistants, the congregation, need covering. Hence the whole business of building, first of all to cover the altar and then the people.[25]

In Gill's view, the church building exists for the altar, to enable the commodious offering of the Sacrifice upon it. With that principle established, he next elaborates on the spatial relationship between altar and church:

Now there is nothing whatever in the nature of an altar that implies that it should be anywhere but in the middle. It began as a table around which people sat and partook of the consecrated bread and wine. It remains that thing. But we may go further and say that not only is the altar a table, but it is a representation of Calvary—the place upon which Christ, the bread and wine, offered Himself. Hence the congruity of the

---

25 Eric Gill, "Mass for the Masses," *Sacred & Secular*, (London, 1940), 146–147.

crucifix on or above this table, heraldically to designate the altar as a Christian one. And as Calvary itself was surrounded by the people who witnessed the crucifixion, so we must suppose the altar should be surrounded by the people when at the Elevation the priest symbolically repeats the act of Christ.[26]

Gill adopts the same dubious assumption as O'Connor about the table of the Last Supper and, by extension, the primitive Eucharistic table: that all were seated around it. For both O'Connor and Gill, the dubiousness of their premise undermines to some degree their assertions about the proper place of the altar and orientation of the priest.

However, Gill seems to depart from O'Connor on the matter of the altar crucifix. Gill sees the crucifix at the altar to be a fitting sign of the true nature of the Christian altar. However, O'Connor will have none of it. In the section *Altar I* in *Liturgy*, O'Connor asserts that "the Crucifix upon the altar for Mass is a grave contravention of the great rubric and tradition of the Roman Church, which bars all emblems of the Passion from the Real Presence."[27] He offers a theological rationale for this view, namely that,

> the Eucharist precedes Calvary in point of time and even of importance, and follows it up for ever, so that Calvary is an episode of the Eucharist and is *inside* the Institution. This is the Priesthood according to the order of Melchisedeck. But we got to thinking that without a crucifix on the altar the Consecration would somehow not be valid. Such is the power of crass ignorance that

---

26 Ibid., 147.

27 A distinction should be noted between a fixed or hanging crucifix in the vicinity of the altar, and a portable crucifix on the altar itself, which would have generally been removed for exposition or benediction.

we have would-be affecting pictures of a priest raising the chalice towards a shadowy crucifixion.

Gill is possibly influenced as much by his Distributist[28] views as by liturgical tradition. He laments the "scandal" that Christianity has become "the religion of a few," but that it "should be to a large extent the religion of the respectable and well-to-do makes the matter worse."[29] He finds a "state of contradiction" between Christianity, on the one hand, as "the religion of God made man, the poor man, the common man, the working man, and on the other the curiously ornate churches, the elaborately robed priests and unintelligibly elaborate ceremonies...a display of worldly grandeur...which seems to display an alliance between the Church and the very Mammon condemned in the Gospels."[30] His sensitivities as a craftsman are further scandalized by churches and their liturgical and decorative accoutrements having become "like everything else in our world, the product of our industrial commercial system, machine-made mass products, imitation antique, whether gothic or classic, in fact not made by man but simply merchandise — stuff produced solely for the profit of investors of capital."[31] Since the Church has "lost the masses" it must reclaim them, and central to this urgent mission is that,

> [t]he altar must be brought back again into the middle of our churches, in the middle of the

---

28 Distributism is a school of economic thought inspired by the social teaching of Pope Leo XIII, that advocates the widespread ownership of the means of production, with the fundamental right of private ownership serving a just social order. It opposed both laissez-faire capitalism and state socialism. G. K. Chesterton and Hilaire Belloc were its principal apostles. Chesterton employed Eli Hamshire's slogan, "three acres and a cow," to advocate every individual's entitlement to own what he needs to live by, and it came to be associated with the Chestertonian Distributist movement of the 1920s.

29 Gill, "Mass for the Masses", 143.

30 Ibid., 144–145.

31 Ibid., 145.

congregation, surrounded by the people — and the word, surrounded, must be taken literally. It is essential that the people be on all sides, in front and behind. The Holy Sacrifice must be offered thus, and in relation to this reform nothing else matters.[32]

Gill's debt to O'Connor is evident in a quotation from *Liturgy*, which includes the quotation marks but does not cite the source:

The liturgy must be revived; revived, i.e. made alive again. But 'to revive the liturgy it is first necessary to disinter it'.[33]

Indeed, Gill at times reveals himself to be very much the disciple of O'Connor. Referring to Langtry-Langton's 1937 article in the journal *The Parthenon*, Gill writes to O'Connor that,

It seems to me that what you said, as quoted in the article, is the whole law and the prophets on the subject of the liturgical revival. I am at present completely one-eyed about it. I see no hope whatever of any such revival until the Mass is brought away from the mystery mongering of obscure sanctuaries separated from the people by rows of clergy and stuff. I don't believe a single atom of good will be done by teaching people the Chant or talking about vestments or Church images until what you have done at the Church of the Holy Martyrs is done everywhere.[34]

32 Ibid., 152.
33 Ibid., 149.
34 Eric Gill, Letter to O'Connor (15 March 1937), in *Letters*, #273: 384.

This almost master-disciple relationship emerged into view again when Gill sent a copy of "Mass for the Masses" to O'Connor, "for your criticism and [I] hope you will approve of it. I should be very grateful if you will tell me where it is in error."[35]

Gill followed faithfully in O'Connor's steps when designing the church of Saint Peter in Gorleston-on-Sea in Norfolk, his only church design. Work on the church began in 1938, when Gill was reading O'Connor's *Liturgy* and submitting his own writing to O'Connor for approbation. Similar to the original plan for O'Connor's First Martyrs, Saint Peter's is a cruciform church with the altar located beneath the central tower.

THE VALUE OF "LITURGY"

Now that death has rendered him permanently safe from episcopal censure, if any indeed would be incurred in our day, O'Connor's liturgical jeremiad merits attention from those interested in the Liturgical Movement, and in the reforms of the Catholic liturgy enacted from the 1950s onwards. O'Connor is notable beyond being the inspiration for Chesterton's beloved Father Brown. As a well-educated, well-read parish priest he was *au fait* with the development of liturgical thinking and the realities of life in parishes, the proposed beneficiaries of any liturgical reform. While his lack of formal liturgical study leads him astray at times, it also means he can think independently of the agenda of the professional liturgists.

---

35   Eric Gill, Letter to O'Connor (28 February 1938), in *Letters*, #287: 400. In this letter, Gill reveals that his article arose from work at Blundell's School for their chapel: "The head master said to me 'Would the altar look better a few feet away from the East wall?', and I said to him 'It doesn't matter where it would look better, the question is where it would *be* better, and where it would be better, you will come to see that it looks better,' and so on. Arising out of this I had to go to Blundell's and given the boys a lecture on 'Christian Altars', of which this paper is the substance" (400).

As the product of an intelligent priest with significant experience of the realities of parish life, O'Connor's *Liturgy* offers an insight into what some of his confreres may also have been thinking, as well as those in his wider circle. It clearly resonated with some leading Catholic figures, including Eric Gill and the superiors of that unnamed religious house in the whose refectory *Liturgy* was read aloud. In this light, O'Connor's voice deserves to be considered along with the better-known and more established voices of liturgical thinking in England. The prescience of many of his opinions is noteworthy. *Liturgy* confirms that there was some liturgical discomfort beyond professional liturgists before the Second Vatican Council, a discomfort the Council Fathers sought to address.

Furthermore, admirers of Chesterton's Father Brown may find interesting, if perhaps astounding, the voice of the man who inspired this beloved character. While his violent opinions may surprise them, his humour should amuse them, even if it is more vigorous than they might have expected from Chesterton's "dull as a Norfolk dumpling" priestly sleuth. After reading *Liturgy* Father Brown fans might find the twinkle in his eye has a new radiance.

Liturgy is an enjoyable read, not least due to the author being so amusingly, unapologetically, provocatively, and breathlessly opinionated. O'Connor is not always a sure guide on matters of liturgical fact but the general sweep of his opinions is of interest as a moment in the history of the last century's liturgical reform, and an enlightening complement to any study of the growing awareness of liturgical reform evident in the letters and articles in English Catholic press from the 1930s onwards.

In conclusion, a reflection from 1948 offers an insight into the quality Chesterton saw in O'Connor that moved him to conceive "Father Brown," and points to the early birth of the disdain in which O'Connor held superficial show and "servants masquerading as masters" which characterises *Liturgy*:

> It is characteristic of the original of "Father Brown" that he rates his detective powers as slight, and sees little justification in having been staged for the part. But we can trust the intuitive powers of Chesterton in his choice. Chesterton was impressed when Father O'Connor told him that, as a boy at his English school, he had the gift of "seeing through" the poses and the pretenses of the new boys. He was able to gauge how much in their behaviour was artificial and put on especially to impress, and what was genuine beneath the outward show.[36]

THE TEXT

The text is reproduced faithfully from the original tract. Most of O'Connor's idiosyncrasies in formatting, typography, and punctuation have been retained as authentic to both the author and his day. Obvious typographical errors in the original printing have been corrected. The content has not been corrected with regard to errors of fact, or assertions that would be contested today. O'Connor should be received as he presented himself; his authentic voice must not be edited out. Any detailed disputing of O'Connor's assertions must take place elsewhere, though his weaknesses are acknowledged in the notes, which will perhaps be of more interest to the non-specialist in liturgy.

Hugh Somerville Knapman OSB
St Elizabeth's, Scarisbrick

---

36 Edward J. Kubaitis, quoted in "News and Comments", *The Chesterton Review* 15, no.1 (February 1986): 118.

BIBLIOGRAPHY

Ahrens, Christian. "Richard Wagner's Twelve Organ Pipes." *The Galpin Society Journal* 50, (March 1997): 212–17.

Bishop, Edmund. *Liturgica Historica: Papers on the Liturgy and Religious Life of the Western Church.* Oxford: Clarendon Press, 1918.

Bradley, George. "A Brief History of the Parish of First Martyrs." In *Consecration Ceremony of the Church of Our Lady and the First Martyrs.* Bradford, 1974.

Chappell, David M. "The Development of the Sanctuary and its Furnishings from Early Christian Times to the Present Day." MA Thesis. University of Sheffield, 1963.

Collins, Judith. *Eric Gill: The Sculpture.* New York: Overlook Press, 1998.

Comper, J. Ninian. *Of the Christian Altar and the Buildings Which Contain It.* London: Society for Promoting Christian Knowledge, 1950.

Corrigan, Felicitas. "The Prescience of Father Brown." *The Clergy Review* (February 1972): 83–95.

Dix, Gregory. *The Shape of the Liturgy.* Westminster: Dacre Press, 1945.

Dognin, Paul Dominique. "L'énigme du «Mysterium Fidei»: À Propos de l'Ancienne Formule Consécratoire du Vin" in *Revue Des Sciences Philosophiques et Théologiques* 92, no.1 (2008): 77–85.

Duchesne, Louis. *Christian Worship: Its Origin and Evolution: A Study of the Latin Liturgy up to the Time of Charlemagne,* 5th Edition. Translated by M. L. McLure. London: Society for Promoting Christian Knowledge, 1919.

Eisenhofer, Ludwig and Joseph Lechner. *The Liturgy of the Roman Rite.* Translated by A. J. and E. F. Peeler. Edited by H. E. Winstone. Edinburgh-London: Nelson, 1961.

Fortescue, Adrian. *The Mass: A Study of the Roman Liturgy,* 3rd Edition. London: Longmans, Green & Co., 1926.

Giles, Richard. *Re-pitching the Tent: Re-ordering the Church Building for Worship and Mission.* Collegeville, MN: The Liturgical Press, 1999.

Gill, Eric. *Sacred & Secular in Art and Industry,* London: J. M. Dent & Sons, 1940.

Harris, Max. *Sacred Folly: A New History of the Feast of Fools.* Ithaca: Cornell University Press, 2011.

Jungmann SJ, Joseph A. *The Early Liturgy to the Time of Gregory the Great.* Translated by Francis A. Brunner. Notre Dame: University of Notre Dame Press, 1959.

___. *The Mass of the Roman Rite: Its Origins and Development.* Translated by Francis A. Brunner Vols. 1 and 2. Notre Dame: University of Notre Dame Press, 2012.

Langtry-Langton, Jack H. "The Church of the First Martyrs, Bradford." *The Parthenon* (March 1937): 195–198.

___. "The Architect Remembers." In *Consecration Ceremony of the Church of Our Lady and the First Martyrs.* Bradford, 1974: 30–32.

Langtry-Langton, Peter. "The Architecture of the Round Church." *1935–1985 Golden Jubilee: The Church of Our Lady and the First Martyrs*, 1985: 14–17.

Mazza, Enrico. *The Eucharistic Prayers of the Roman Rite.* Collegeville: The Liturgical Press, 1989.

O'Connor, John. "Old Douai." *The Douai Magazine* 15, no. 1 (Spring 1948): 8–12.

___. As "Father Brown", *A Month of Sundays: The Foolishness of Father Brown.* Bradford: T. Geoghegan, no date.

O'Shea, William J. *The Worship of the Church.* London: Darton, Longman & Todd, 1957.

Parsch, Pius. *The Liturgy of the Mass.* 3rd Edition. Translated by H. E. Winstone. London: B. Herder, 1957.

Pocknee, Cyril Edward. *The Christian Altar in History and Today.* London: A. R. Mowbray, 1963.

Shewring Walter., ed., *The Letters of Eric Gill.* London: Jonathan Cape, 1947.

Smith, Julia. *The Elusive Father Brown: The Life of Mgr John O'Connor.* Leominster: Gracewing, 2010.

Theisen, Reinold. "Saint Peter the Mass Liturgist According to the Council of Trent." *Archivum Historiae Pontificiae*, Vol. 5 (1967): 345–354.

Turner, Cuthbert H. "Notes on the 'Apostolic Constitutions': The Text of the Eighth Book." *The Journal of Theological Studies* 31, no. 122 (1930): 128–141.

Wagner, Peter. *Einführung in die gregorianischen Melodien; ein Handbuch der Choral wissenschaft*, Vol. 2. Leipzig: Druck und Verlag von Breitkopf & Härtel, 1912.

Photo 1: Sketch of O'Connor's proposed new church in Heights Lane, Bradford, under the title originally conceived for it, by its architect, Jack Langtry-Langton. (Archives of Our Lady and First Martyrs)

Photo 2: The church of Our Lady and First Martyrs in its early days. (Archives of Our Lady and First Martyrs)

Photo 3: Street elevation of Our Lady and First Martyrs not long after opening. (Archives of Our Lady and First Martyrs)

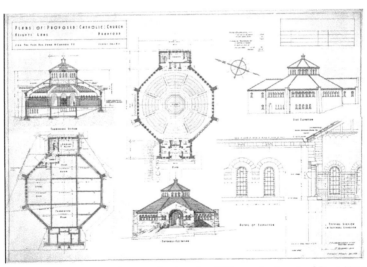

Photo 4: Jack Langtry-Langton's plans for O'Connor's church of First Martyrs (opened 1935)

Photo 5: "On the dotted line"—Monsignor John O'Connor in his latter years. (Leeds Diocesan Archives)

Photo 6: The interior of Our Lady and First Martyrs in early 2020. (Photograph by the editor)

Photo 7: North elevation of Our Lady and First Martyrs in early 2020, showing an entrance to the hall beneath the church. (Photograph by the editor)

WHY REVIVE THE LITURGY, AND HOW?

INTRODUCTION

How came I to say these things? How came I to have them to say? For nearly sixty years the Liturgy has been dearer to me than eyesight, space or liberty, and I have received my reward in millions of ecstatic moments: indeed it has been the bait by which God has hooked me, and the hook endures though the bait has melted away. Only twice in twenty years have I sung High Mass. Only once in twenty years have I taken part in Solemn Mass with Ministers. It is over forty-three years since I assisted at a Solemn Festal Office. I have seen Public Worship becoming more and more hopelessly private and peculiar, and now I am in a position to state that Public Worship does not exist. There are certain apologies for Public Worship which are mistaken for the genuine article, and of these I hope to take notice as we go on. Such repetitions as may occur in the course of the essay are made for the sake of clearness.

ON REVIVING THE LITURGY

What is the Liturgy which we would revive? Benediction is not the Liturgy: neither is Solemn Vespers nor Compline. The Divine Office (no matter how solemnly performed) cannot be classed as Public Worship, neither is it something in between. It is a solemnisation of private prayer. We are faced with this curious dilemma—that in one age of the Church there were no morning services, and in a still longer space there were no evening services. Is it necessary to show how fasting [for] Communion forced the evening Liturgy into the first hours of the morning? For centuries after this had taken place there was no evening service, unless it were in churches where those on whom it devolved would go through Evensong or Compline, or would even anticipate Matins and Lauds, according to their constitutions. But Matins, and Lauds and Little Hours have almost invariably been the private prayers of a community. Compared with

3

the breaking of the bread all these things can be classed as trimmings—beautiful trimmings, which it would break some of our hearts to go without, but not necessary by necessity of precept, unless you allow the Emperor Justinian to be of Divine institution.[1]

The Liturgy is essentially and exclusively the solemn sacrifice of the Mass and nothing else. Do you require proof? See how Holy Church inserts all her Acts into the body of the Mass. Even weddings and funerals are embodied in this grand Act which we call the Liturgy, so that when we speak of reviving the Liturgy we speak of reviving the public celebration of Mass. What we are accustomed to call Low Mass is a very beautiful and singularly perfect thing in itself, and from Low Mass again must radiate the revival of the Liturgy.

You cannot revive public worship until you have disinterred it, and it is buried a thousand fathoms deep. It is like a primeval forest long since turned to stone, and turned upside down and inside out by the convulsions of ages and long lapses of memory, and well-meaning souls are now wasting boxes of matches trying to set it on fire.

I see in our Catholic newspapers endless free discussions, more or less solemn, in the correspondence columns, as to how much private devotion is permissible in public worship, or how much is possible, or desirable, and so on. We have almost an official movement to provide all the holy people of God with Missals in the vernacular, so that in our mighty imitation cathedrals the vast majority who can neither see nor hear may arrive at understanding what they read. We are indeed sick of the palsy. Why go to church to read a Missal?

---

1   Presumably Emperor Justinian I's edict in 528 imposing the obligation on clergy appointed to churches to celebrate the Divine Office, in particular the morning and evening offices. The Divine Office/Liturgy of the Hours was originally "the affair of the individual...[and] the liturgical Hours sprang from this private regime of prayer" (Josef Jungmann SJ, *The Early Liturgy to the Time of Gregory the Great* [Notre Dame: University of Notre Dame Press,1959], 105).

Such public worship as we are permitted is dutifully practised by the women, but by the men under increasing protest.
In many of the churches of Spain before the cataclysm, men
(I am credibly informed) were conspicuous by their absence:
in fact three young men from this parish of mine told me
that on entering a large Spanish church at Santiago for Sunday Mass they created such a sensation that the Mass for a
time was quite ignored.

> I have assisted in the Choir
> In the next stall to the Prior,

and though I know the Holy Week Services by heart, I
could not at any given moment, for the life of me, say what
they were at round the altar. Behind, about five steps down,
was the congregation, and I leave to your imagination how
much they saw of it. The singing was quite of the finest,
but no sound was uttered by the congregation. So mature
consideration convinces me that in the celebration of Mass
for the people everything is so wrong that it cannot be any
worse, and to revive the Liturgy seems to me to mean for
certain good people some wild exaggeration of one or other
of the various wrongnesses.

The time has to be in the early part of the day because of
the strict fast before Communion. So strict is this reputed
to be that I have known cases of invalids who never could
receive Holy Communion except immediately after Midnight
Mass of Christmas. Wise legislation has, of course, modified
all this,[2] but there are servants who are still more zealous
than their masters, and long to "glory in our flesh," as Saint
Paul says. But the everlasting uniform pressure of fasting

---

2 At the time O'Connor wrote the obligation to fast from all food and
drink before receiving Holy Communion commenced at midnight that began
the day of reception. This long-standing discipline was modified in the 1917
Code of Canon Law, with Canon 858 allowing those with long-term illness
to receive Communion even if they had taken medicine or water beforehand.

communion has driven Solemn Worship into a corner. Such modifications as strict fast from alcoholic drink, or say a natural fast of three hours before celebration or Communion, would be a step towards renewing the face of the earth.[3]

I think Solemn Mass once a month at 6, 7 or 8 o'clock on a Sunday evening would make it easy for quite large sections of the working-class to put in an appearance — easier for them than it is now, when from Saturday noon to Sunday is all they get of real free time. So much for the hour of Mass.

Now for the language. I agree thoroughly with Father Martindale[4] that it would break my heart to abandon Latin, and so I would keep the Ordinary of the Mass, excluding the sung portions, in Latin, especially as I think the Latin of the Canon is our inheritance from Saint Peter himself.[5] Latin, so

---

3   O'Connor's advocacy for a reduction of the Eucharistic fast to three hours would be answered after his death with Pius XII's 1957 *motu proprio, Sacram Communionem*. Paul VI would reduce it to one hour before Communion in November 1964, the discipline which holds today.

4   Father Cyril Charles Martindale SJ (1879–1963) wrote on the subject of the vernacular in the Mass, in a letter to the *Catholic Herald* on 23 July 1937, and in an article the same year published by the Jesuit journal *The Month*: "Sunday Mass and the Vernacular," *The Month* 170, no.879 (September 1937): 261–267. In the letter to the *Catholic Herald* he wrote: "Personally, I am clear. I understand Latin; I love it — its sounds, its construction — everything else to do with it. Selfishly, I should hate its translation into non-Latin tongues... All the same, I think that Latin should be given up in our non-sacrificial prayers. I like everything in Latin: but that is my fad. I feel that everything that is not Sacrificial, or essentially Official, should be in the living language of the Laity... I am not, week by week, being married, let alone baptised, or even buried. Yet local ladies and gentlemen are. They may as well know what is happening." In his piece in *The Month* Martindale distinguishes between "the 'sacrificial' part of Mass and the 'instructional,' praise-and-prayer part. We are, therefore, leagues from simply suggesting that the whole Liturgy should be in the vernacular. We should hate it. On the other hand, we are quite sure that most English Catholics are quite unaware of the progress the idea is making abroad." (263) His conclusion opens with the caution that "I think that there never was a time more inopportune that our own for the change which is advocated" (266).

5   While O'Connor seems to distinguish Petrine inheritance from Petrine composition with regard to the Roman Canon, ascribing the Latin version to Saint Peter was idiosyncratic. At the Council of Trent, even the most fervent

long as I can remember, has been to me a living language, that is to say the impact of the words is direct to my senses.

Here again, let us beware of the servants who take mastership upon themselves. It seems to be the badge of the servile mind — the wanting to "boss" someone. It is merely thin rubbish to say that the use of the vernacular would obscure theological meanings. Better have them obscured than non-existent. Besides all the languages in which Mass is said now were once vernacular and never saved any theological meaning that we know of. If you must have a noble alien medium of Solemn Worship why not go back to the Hebrew of the Temple, or the Aramaic of the Supper Room? The Latin which we use is the cheapest vernacular that could be obtained in 500 years. So is the Greek: so is the Slavonic. Besides I am very mindful that the words of consecration in every Liturgy are obviously handed down by word of mouth, and not by the written word. We have a monument of this in our Latin Consecration of the Chalice. The words "Mystery of Faith" are not found in any other Liturgy except the original vernacular of Palestine, and then they occur in the Consecration of the Host.[6]

---

advocate of Petrine composition of the Roman Canon, the Jesuit Francisco Torres, held that the Roman Canon was a translation from Greek. Trent contented itself with merely affirming the apostolic origin of the Mass. The Roman Canon in O'Connor's day was almost identical with that used in the time of Pope Saint Gregory the Great (†604). St. Gregory himself ascribed the Canon to a certain *scholasticus*, whom most scholars would identify as a single editor (not a composer). The majority of the Roman Canon was in place by the death of Pope Damasus (†384). cf. R. Theisen, "Saint Peter the Mass Liturgist According to the Council of Trent," *Archivum Historiae Pontificiae* Vol. 5 (1967): 345–354; William J. O'Shea, *The Worship of the Church* (London: Darton, Longman & Todd, 1960), 375–380; Joseph A. Jungmann, *The Mass of the Roman Rite: Its Origins and Development*, vol. 1, trans. Francis A. Brunner (Notre Dame: University of Notre Dame Press, 2012), 49ff; Enrico Mazza, *The Eucharistic Prayers of the Roman Rite* (Collegeville, MN: The Liturgical Press, 1989), 57–58.

6   O'Connor seems to have in mind Book VIII of the Apostolic Constitutions (375–380), where the words *Hoc est mysterium novi testamenti* are said in the

I have read with varying degrees of amusement thousands of words arguing all round this little point. The secret is that the first Syrian Pope[7] (trusting to memory, of course) used his own Liturgy in the Holy Roman Church. His priests con-celebrating picked up this peculiarity "Mystery of Faith," and in after years, it is lawful to surmise, slipped it into the Consecration of the Chalice, since it could not be noticed among so many other words.[8]

A piece of irritating nonsense which was given out quite freely when I was anxious about these matters is the reason for the secret utterance of the greater part of the Liturgy. We were

---

consecration of the Host. The Constitutions are now held to be of Syrian/ Antiochene origin though a Palestinian origin was allowed for the first six books. cf. C. H. Turner, "Notes on the 'Apostolic Constitutions': The Text of the Eighth Book," *The Journal of Theological Studies* 31, no. 122 (1930): 130; O'Shea, *Worship of the Church*, 107; Ludwig Eisenhofer and Joseph Lechner, *The Liturgy of the Roman Rite*, trans. A. J. and E. F. Peeler and ed. H. E. Winstone (Nelson, Edinburgh-London, 1961), 254.

7   Presumably St Anicetus, pope from 155–166.

8   The origins and purpose of the phrase *mysterium fidei*, "the mystery of faith," inserted into the formula of consecration over the chalice in the ancient Roman Canon, are uncertain. They first appear in the commentary on the Gallican Mass by St. Germanus (†576) but are not found in the earliest record of the substantially-complete Roman Canon in St. Ambrose's *De Sacramentis* (387). One theory holds that Pope Leo the Great inserted the words to emphasize the value of the chalice in opposition to the Manicheans who refused to receive from the chalice. Pope Innocent III held that they attested to the Real Presence. Another theory holds that the words are derived from 1 Timothy 3:9, 13, which refers to deacons "holding the mystery of faith," which is Christ's act of faith on the Cross. In the Mass the deacon is the proper minister of the chalice and elevates it at the conclusion of the Canon. Some even hold that the deacon originally said these words, addressing the congregation. The phrase was relocated in the new missal of 1970 to just after the consecration of the chalice, though no longer connected specifically to the chalice but to the Paschal Mystery. In the first days of the 1970 reform at Douai Abbey, the words were proclaimed by the deacon until an instruction returned them to the celebrant. Cf. Jungmann, *Mass of the Roman Rite*, vol. 2, 199–201; Eisenhofer and Lechner, *Liturgy of the Roman Rite*, 315; Paul Dominique Dognin, "L'énigme du «Mysterium Fidei»: À Propos de l'Ancienne Formule Consécratoire du Vin" *Revue Des Sciences Philosophiques et Théologiques* 92, no. 1 (2008): 77–85.

told cock-and-bull stories about the discipline of the secret. No attempt was made to reconcile this secrecy with the fact that all those who were not in the secret were already gone out.[9]

Note. — It is plain to me that the whole secrecy of the Canon of the Mass was brought about by the ostentations of the singers and the failure of the office of Deacon, simultaneous with the institution of the Sacred College of Cardinals.[10]

One of the first steps to restoring the Celebration of the Mass as Public Worship will be to restore the office of Deacon. It should be the Deacon's office, above all, to lead the congregation in its vernacular responses to the Celebrant.[11] Needless to say extreme holiness of life coupled

---

9 That is, the catechumens et al, who were dismissed before the Offertory, at the end of the first half of the Mass, 'The Mass of the Catechumens.' O'Connor has in mind, of course, the silent, or *sotto voce*, recitation of most of the second half of the Mass, 'The Mass of the Faithful,' which Browning famously described as "the blessed mutter of the Mass" in his poem, "The Bishop Orders his Tomb at Saint Praxed's Church." The silent recitation of the canon dates from the seventh century, though the dismissal of the catechumens had ceased by the beginning of that century. Moreover, the secrecy of *disciplina arcani* does not appear till the third century. cf. Jungmann, *Early Liturgy*, 159; Pius Parsch, *The Liturgy of the Mass* (London: B. Herder, 1957), 202, 229. O'Shea suggests that the silence of the canon reflects the change of emphasis from a sacrifice of praise going up to God, to the coming down in mystery of God's gift to humanity, in *Worship of the Church*, 380-381.

10 The office of cardinal emerges into historical clarity in the latter half of the first millennium. Of the three classes of cardinal — cardinal bishop, cardinal priest, cardinal deacon — the cardinal deacons are the earliest, with a lineage tracing from the ordination of the first seven deacons in Acts 6 through to the seven deacons who administered the patrimony of the Church in the city of Rome. Though invariably priests not deacons by ordination, cardinal deacons wear dalmatics when liturgically assisting the pope. In the Roman Mass of early centuries, the deacons had significant roles to play, especially in the preparation of the gifts for the sacrifice and ministering at the altar during the canon through to the rite of communion. Presumably O'Connor has in mind the advent of the Low Mass at which there were no deacons or subdeacons who took cues from the words of the celebrant. Moreover, as the Sanctus and Benedictus chants became longer they were often sung by the choir during the Canon, making the priest's audibility redundant.

11 Jungmann notes that the deacon was replaced by lesser clerics very early on, "for his duty as prayer-leader for the people was never much developed;"

with tone-deafness should not be the essential qualification for this office. Any educated man of decent life and good repute, inured to the sound of his own voice, would do. Why not convert clergymen? Some feel it a cruel privation to be of no assistance in Public Worship. They could be Masters of the Musick.

CHURCH MUSIC

> O Music! Music! though you wake in me
> No Joy, no Joy at all.[12]

Ah, Music! What crimes are committed in thy name! We do not read in the Gospel that Saint Peter (or any of the others) was called by the Lord because of his musical acquirements, though James and John, being of the priestly caste, must have had some notion of the Temple music. I have a feeling (purely subjective) that Saint Paul had no ear for music, though he advises us to "make melody in our hearts to God," but this does not go beyond private worship.

How did music get into public worship? There was no need for it at the beginning, and presently it would have been very dangerous, as betraying the whereabouts of the hunted sect. As Chesterton says, "When the eagle soars the singing birds are dumb." Why does the Roman Church cherish the tradition that Saint Cecily introduced music into public worship in Rome? I explain it to myself in this way. She arose at a period when the Emperor was fading from Rome, and her ancient house, standing much as it did, became rendezvous of a larger congregation than was customary. Here

---

Mass of the Roman Rite, vol.1, 208. The deacon as prayer-leader was more developed in the East where he was a bridge between "the priest at the altar and the assembled congregation," leading them in vernacular prayers while the celebrant was at his work at the altar. cf. Jungmann, *Early Liturgy,* 216.
12   From Francis Thompson's poem "The Dread of Height" (1897).

it was found that the public worship of a large crowd had to be sustained by some kind of monotone. The monotone itself requires to be tuned and kept together by an agreed change of note at the end of a phrase, and a bigger change at the end of a sentence.[13] Even a small number of more or less civilised persons having to speak in concert will spontaneously evolve this system, as children do saying prayers at school. Now in monasteries, where this custom is essential and habitual, they put down a note on the organ to keep the new boys up to pitch. This is my conjecture about Saint Cecily: that she invented an organ — quite a simple instrument — to keep up the note for the congregation.[14] I see that the late lamented Richard Wagner constructed an organ to maintain the chord of E flat during the first hundred and fifty bars of the "Rheingold."[15] Does not history repeat itself?

Now it is found that this mode of chanting is excellent for the voice, because it builds a bridge from the speaking to the singing voice, and beautifies the speaking voice without making it sensual; in fact it is an anti-sensual blend. Austerity is one of the keys to beauty — it is the least dispensable of all the ingredients in beauty. An unbalanced aesthetic sense is the enemy of all stateliness and beauty in public worship, because it is predominantly sensual, and the sensual destroys beauty by making it first lovely, then sticky, then stuffy; and last of all it is ugly. It amuses me to

---

13 The description matches that of the method for the recitation of readings and prayers said aloud by a minister rather than congregational signing. This "accentuated reading" is described by L. Duchesne in *Christian Worship: Its Origin and Evolution: A Study of the Latin Liturgy up to the Time of Charlemagne*, 5th Edition, trans. M. L. McLure (London: Society for Promoting Christian Knowledge, 1919), 117–118.

14 St. Cecilia (†230) did not invent the organ, and her association with music dates from the Renaissance. The organ myth seems to derive from a misreading of *organis* in the Acts recounting her martyrdom.

15 Presumably the one for the performance at Bayreuth on 13 August 1876. cf. Christian Ahrens, "Richard Wagner's Twelve Organ Pipes," *The Galpin Society Journal* 50 (March, 1997): 212–217.

see newspaper correspondents bemiring themselves through column after column, just like the sailor and Caliban in "The Tempest," whilst many an amateur choir should be arrested for brawling in a place of worship.[16]

Church music is always growing to a semi-permanent atrocity, because the average sensual man will never perceive or admit this elementary fact. Let us examine more closely. As a boy I learned the Mechlin version of Gregorian. All the bits I adored had to be dropped when I learned the Ratisbon version. In due course I found that my darling Mechlin was bad music, and the Ratisbon variant (for the most part) scholarly and sound. But in the Solesmes or the Vatican version I found all the worst errors put back. I enquired of two first-rate scholars why this should be, and they both agreed that it was because the French monks ignored foreign sources. We owe incalculable thanks to them none the less for their restoration of the right manner and spirit of Gregorian singing.[17]

One of the two authorities consulted pointed out how the Cistercians introduced Neums and made Gregorian Propers the department of specialists, and no small specialists at

---

16 O'Connor had little patience for the imperfections of choirs. His biographer reports that his parish choir often "got the sharp end of his tongue," with former choristers recalling how "he was quite likely to turn from the altar and demand they 'stop that bloody row' as he wasn't able to concentrate on the Mass" (Julia Smith, *The Elusive Father Brown* (Leominster: Gracewing, 2010), 75.
17 Reflecting the increasing liturgical awareness of the nineteenth century, revised approaches to Gregorian chant were put forward in many new editions of the book of Mass chants called the *Graduale*. The Mechlin edition, published in 1848, was a new edition of the Medicean *Graduale* of 1614, which was a delayed fruit of the Council of Trent. The Mechlin edition was widely adopted in France, which explains its use at Douai. The 1871 Ratisbon edition was a re-editing of the Medicean. Meanwhile new discoveries in chant were being made at Solesmes Abbey but held in check by the privileged status granted to the Ratisbon edition. On 22 November 1903, Pius X issued an Instruction on Sacred Music, *Tra le sollecitudini*, which saw the creation of a commission in 1904, leading to the publication of the official *Graduale Romanum* in 1908, embodying the pioneering work of Dom Pothier at Solesmes.

that! Within a generation or so commonsense rejected it
all and put in Sequences to make sense. (Note at once the
conflict between mere loveliness and intellectual beauty.)
At another stage of our development we dropped a lot of
Sequences without restoring the Neums, and now in the
new restoration we restore the Neums without dropping the
Sequences.[18] This is—

> A process of cancelling themselves out
> Much favoured by the unco' devout.[19]

But it has played the very devil with public worship.[20]

Need I go on to note the magnificent development of
classical polyphony, the father of all symphonic music,
instrumental as well as vocal? When they combined the
vocal band with the instrumental band the Vienna School

---

18   Neums, the method of musical notation for plainchant, and sequences,
which originally took up melodic motifs in the Alleluia chant, both predate
the Cistercians and have a Benedictine origin. The few sequences in modern use are sacred poems with a repeating melody, regular metre, and often
rhyming in their texts. O'Connor might perhaps be overstating in a polemical
way the work of the early Cistercians in developing chant books for use
throughout their order to ensure a common observance, free of the Benedictine "excesses" which they held to be decadent, according to Peter Wagner in
his *Einführung in die gregorianischen Melodien; ein Handbuch der Choral wissenschaft,*
vol.2 (Leipzig, 1912), 291f.

19   *Unco* is Scots idiom for "very." The source of the apparent quotation
was not traced by the editor.

20   Sr Margaret Truran has given a happy example of this from an entry in the
house chronicle of Stanbrook Abbey for the clothing of Sr. Gertrude Casanova
on 20 October 1892: "As no relatives or friends could be present, Mrs. Casanova
desired there should be a good number of our Fathers who were to come at her
expense. Dr. Scarisbrick, Abbot President [*a monk of Douai*], all Malvern Fathers
[*from the Douai daughter house in Malvern*], several from St Michael's [*Belmont
Priory, at that time a common novitiate and house of studies for the English Benedictine
Congregation*] with some Juniors, & other Fathers, all Benedictines—about
twenty in all. The Pontifical Vespers were splendid, chanted in two choirs,
viz. the Monks chanting Mechlin & our Choir Dom Pothier! D. Laurentia at
the Organ made both go very well & the contrast was not discordant. The 'Jesu
Corona' [*hymn for virgins*] was Mechlin on both sides; the Magnificat D. Pothier,
as likewise the Antiphons. In fact all the chant was excellent."

of Church Music[21] was born and specialists ceased to exist, while professionals took their place. Then the professional became a hireling; then the music with all its beauty perforce had to be abolished as being neither public worship nor private devotion.

(Here I may add a note more or less personal. In the course of my experience of this school of music I found opening at my feet dismaying depths of vulgarity even in such pious composers as Gounod. But there was worse to come, since the most vulgar composers of all wrote easy Masses for easy-going performers whose arrogance grew with their incompetence, until frightful scenes were enacted instead of public worship, and the Choir was variously named "The Cock-loft," "The Hen-run" and "The Hullabaloo." Many "Masses" composed for such are hopelessly bad music, intended for voices which cannot dwell in peace with any note, nor with ease on any note.)

From all this we have been delivered by the Motu Proprio of His Holiness,[22] but we are wandering in the wilderness without a Moses, nor even with a Promised Land in sight. Some are not merely harking back to the fleshpots of Egypt but are obtusely abusing the manna in the desert. "Masses" in the musical sense was a technical term for the setting of the Ordinary of the Mass. There never has been a word about the "Proper" because the composers did not know that such a thing existed.[23] The Cistercians made it impossible to sing the Proper, so that even in the new reform the present

---

21   Presumably the First Viennese School of the late eighteenth century.

22   Pius X's *Tra le sollecitudini* of 1903, referred to in note 17 above. In it the pope established plainchant and polyphony as proper to the Mass, and deprecated the "theatrical style" that developed especially in the nineteenth century.

23   Put simply, the Ordinary of the Mass encompasses the unchanging texts of the Mass (both spoken and sung, e.g. Kyrie, Gloria, and Credo), while the Proper refers to those texts that change according to the particular day (e.g. the introit, offertory, and communion chants).

writer has only heard the Proper in monastic and collegiate choirs. A great deal of it is the most beautiful melodic invention ever vouchsafed to man, but it will all have to be swept away before public worship can revive.

Of course what is chiefly wrong with Church music is the words. All the well-meant efforts to teach the people enough Latin for Church purposes are merely the result of profound and incorrigible ignorance; ignorance of the effect and purpose of language, ignorance and carelessness of all consequences. Why not go back to Aramaic?

Now for the Reconstruction. The vernacular of the Litany is our oldest remnant of public worship. Saint Gregory the Great began it in Rome, and it still remains to us as the Kyrie Eleison. Those who have assisted at the Greek Liturgy will remember how frequently the Deacon intones these words. As I interpret the matter, Saint Gregory, fresh from Constantinople, introduced these words in favour of the immense preponderance of poor Greeks in Rome who knew not Latin, so that we have in the Latin Mass itself a monument of vernacular worship.[24] I take it that by Saint Gregory's time Deacons as leaders of the congregation had long ceased to exist, but I notice that the place of the singing schola was right in the middle of the nave so as to be in immediate contact with the congregation.

---

24 The *Kyrie eleison* is the remnant of a litany of petitions that had been a feature of some eastern liturgies, especially of Jerusalem and Antioch, to which children especially were encouraged to give the response *Kyrie eleison*, "Lord, have mercy." Such a litany was a dialogue between clergy and people in making earnest petitions to God, a function recognisable in the modern prayers of the faithful. However, in Rome it was likely to have been introduced under Pope Gelasius (†496). It was recited during processions to stational churches in Rome. Pope Gregory the Great appears to have removed the litany's petitions and added *Christe eleison.* cf. O'Shea, *Worship of the Church*, pp. 323–325. St. Benedict's reference to the "litany" that ends the hours of the Divine Office denotes this simpler *Kyrie*. cf. Eisenhofer and Lechner, *Liturgy of the Roman Rite*, 79–80.

The Litany of the Saints as we have it is of Irish origin, but Saint Gregory had it first from the Greek Church. The Deacons intoned the petitions and the people responded in facsimile. Hence the rule that Litanies must be doubled. This is still done after the blessing of the font. It should be done in every procession, and it is still the rule (even in the private recitation of the Litany) that the first three petitions be duplicated, or there is no indulgence.[25]

I see that in certain Liturgies great Litanies are chanted by the Deacons or Cantors during, for instance, the bridal procession to the altar, after the contract has been solemnised outside the Church. The Introit of the Mass was a very stately business, and the procession recited alternately with the congregation the psalm and antiphon of the day. The priest and the people sang antiphonally the culmination of the Preface in each Mass. This can be seen by anyone who knows that the Sanctus of the Requiem Mass is a simple extension of the Preface. Of course we have changed all that, but was the change so holy that it would be a sacrilege to change back again? Every change that the present writer has been able to ascertain since the time of Saint Gregory has been to the entire undoing of public worship. Only to use the phrase of a devout lady, it has now come to "one quick-firing Mass-priest with the stole about his ears, buzzing like a bee in a bottle." We build our churches larger and larger, so that the majority of people can get away from the noise whilst out of sight of the action.

---

25 The Litany of the Saints represents the re-emergence of the earlier litany form, the invocation of the saints replacing the petitions of the early liturgy. It is used on a number of solemn liturgical occasions, such as ordinations. On Rogation Days and the blessing of churches it accompanies a procession. If there is no procession a litany is said kneeling due to its supplicatory nature. A number of variant litanies had attached to them indulgences, which remitted, either partially or fully, the temporal satisfaction remaining due on sins already forgiven. cf. O'Shea, *Worship of the Church*, 519–524.

Be it enacted, therefore, that there shall be no music in public worship — that is to say in the solemn Liturgy, and that there shall be no Low Mass at any High Altar. I quite agree with the French author who said he knew of nothing more beautiful than Parsifal except any Low Mass you like, in any church you like[26] — but Low Mass is not public worship.[27]

Would I do away with Latin? If the vernacular were specialised enough for public worship I certainly would do away with Latin. Here I distinguish; in all the public parts of public worship I should insist on the vernacular. I should insist on the people taking their full and vocal share in the celebration of the Mass. As a step to this why not revive the original way of concelebration at Lourdes and places where they pilgrim? It would relieve the congestion of say two hundred and seventy-five priests waiting in queue for the chance of one altar in twenty, and it would introduce

26   The French author is the music critic Alfred Ernst (†1898), in particular his sentiments on page 128 of his book *Richard Wagner et le drame contemporain* (Paris, 1887). It is not certain O'Connor would have read this, but he most likely would have read Paul Claudel (†1955), who quotes in his *Richard Wagner — Rêverie d'un poète français* the possibly unattributed reference to Ernst's words by Edouard Dujardin (†1949) in the "latest" issue of the *Revue Wagnerienne.* Claudel's *Rêverie* was written in 1934, at a time when O'Connor was doing serious liturgical thinking as he planned First Martyrs. My thanks to Dr. Brian Sudlow and his colleagues in the Francofil email group for identifying O'Connor's reference.

27   Low Mass, or *Missa lecta* ("read Mass"), has its origins in the emergence of Masses said for small groups or private intentions as early as the third century, and the ritual is scaled down accordingly. O'Connor wants to enhance the ritual but remove the music except for chant, and actively involve the congregation in their spoken parts. O'Connor seems to object to the result described by Jungmann: "With us the private Mass has [become] simply *the* Mass . . . the *missa lecta* as the basic form" (*Mass of the Roman Rite*, vol.1, .229); see also 212ff. O'Shea analyses the reason the faithful came to accept the displacement of the Solemn Mass as the norm: "In practice, men preferred the more tranquil, less complicated, and what they really believed in their hearts to be the more spiritual (because less external), low Mass. This was the attitude that had to be overcome with such great difficulty when the modern liturgical revival tried to revive the true concept of the Mass as a corporate action" (*Worship of the Church*, 133–34).

(God willing) a note of stateliness which has long been absent from High Mass. "Let me congratulate you," said an old priest once to the present writer. "What about?" said I, "It is not my Jubilee!" "No," he said, "but it is the first High Mass I ever seen that was neither a tragedy nor a farce."

"TRAINING COLLEGES"

I am not an archaeologist nor too much enamoured of primitive observances, but I do say that public worship will have to begin all over again. There will have to be an experimental class in public worship for the discarding of useless trimmings, meaningless customs and those pageantries which are not solemn, and the re-moulding of public worship on the lines of public benefit, and until we can build churches more conformable with the restored Liturgy we must eliminate all aesthetic display and go back to the austere beauty of what I may characterise as punctuated Plain Chant. This will train the voices of God's people far better than a guinea a lesson — in fact we shall be beautiful without knowing it, and this is one of the perfect joys. Hence I look forward to an age in which attendance at public worship will be actuated by a much higher and even livelier motive than escape from mortal sin.

Shall we ever realise that Satan's favourite suggestion to all pious clerics is now: If thou be a man of God, command this Bread to be made stones. The true Gregorian music is still existent in the Ambrosian Liturgy[28] and is easy for a congregation, but as for the Roman Gregorian, even before the Cistercian elaborations, the Germans in Rome turned all minor melodies into the Major, as may be seen in the Paschal Ite Missa Est and the Prose de l'Ane,[29] etc., etc.

---

28   The ancient liturgical rite of Milan.
29   The "Prose of the Donkey" was the chant that accompanied the entrance of a girl and an infant boy seated on a donkey, at the medieval Feast of the

Keeping in mind that our original model of the Western Liturgy (in fact where it joins hands with the Eastern) is the Good Friday service, I would have a joyful entrance for Festivals as distinct from the silent, sorrowful one on Good Friday and at Requiem Mass. This entrance as in livelier times could take its colour from the occasion. The Kyrie would not be said or sung at the altar, and the Gloria would never be intoned until after the Communion; it might even be expedient to confine the Gloria to the Bishop himself, as was compulsory in the earliest days.[30] The Gloria is the Angel's Song, and the Bishop is the Angel of the Church;[31] therefore he salutes the congregation after the Gloria with "Pax Vobis," the Angelic salutation as at the first Gloria. This could conclude the solemnity. The artistic sense could expatiate as to whether it were better the Bishop should turn round as he left the church to say the "Pax Vobis" or whether he should chant it from the throne.[32]

VESTMENTS

Before we go into the church at all a few alterations in the priestly vestments seem desirable. Durandus[33] and all

---

Ass on 14 January, which commemorated the Flight into Egypt and was popular in France.

30   The Gloria is a morning hymn originating in the eastern Church which was probably first used in Rome at the Mass of Christmas. Later it was extended by Pope Symmachus (†514) to Mass on Sundays and the feasts of martyrs, but only if a bishop was the celebrant. By the twelfth century it had come to be allowed at festal Masses celebrated by any priest. cf. Jungmann, *Mass of the Roman Rite*, vol.1, 356–357; Duchesne, *Christian Worship*, 166; O'Shea, *Worship of the Church*, 328–334.

31   Revelation 2 addresses to the bishops of various Christian communities as "angels."

32   Until the modern reform, the bishop still turned to the congregation to intone the *Gloria*, a residual reference to the *Gloria* originally being sung by the congregation. cf. O'Shea, *Worship of the Church*, 330.

33   Durandus, or Guillaume Durand (†1296), Bishop of Mende and a noted canonist and liturgical commentator. His *Rationale divinorum officiorum*

fanciful French symbolists can be dismissed with a wave of the hand, and, when the alb is girded, the useless and undecorative maniple can be for ever left in the bottom drawer.[34] It must be taken for granted that the cope is not an Ecclesiastical vestment, but only a protection from the weather.[35] Its common use was necessitated in the Middle Ages by the fact that the nave was often without roof or window. The chasuble must be of the stately and solemn nature that it was in the beginning — the vestment of the Orator or the Sage.[36] There is a statue in the Vatican showing the chasuble in use 300 B. C. That is the kind of chasuble that will be wanted. It will be just as solemn-looking as the cope and much more clear of error. The pallium is worn outside the chasuble and so should be the stole, for stole and pallium are one and the same.[37] (See the Greek Liturgy and all the others which have not been trampled

---

was a compendium of medieval symbolic interpretations of liturgical ritual that was highly influential long after his death.

34   It so happened that the use of the maniple would be made optional by the decree *Tres abhinc annos* of 1967. It is still mandatory in the extraordinary form of the Mass, which uses the missal and rubrics of 1962.

35   The cope is said to derive from the Roman *pluviale*, which was a type of raincoat. O'Connor seems to have been influenced by Edmund Bishop's study of the cope, and its immediate origin in the monastic *cappa clausa*. cf. Edmund Bishop, "Origins of the Cope as a Church Vestment," in *Liturgica Historica: Papers on the Liturgy and Religious Life of the Western Church* (Oxford: Clarendon Press, 1918), 260-275.

36   The chasuble derives from the Roman *paenula*, another outer garment that had come to replace the *toga* in the later Roman empire. The woollen toga was worn only by Roman citizens, and those of senatorial rank wore a more voluminous type. Being expensive and difficult to wash only the wealthy would wear it outside of formal occasions. Originally of semi-elliptical shape which fell about the whole body, with a hole in the middle for the head, it resembled a small house, the reason for its other Latin name *casula*.

37   Both stole and pallium (the latter worn only by metropolitan archbishops) are said, according to one school of thought, to derive from sashes worn by the lower and upper echelons respectively of the Roman civil service as signs of their status. cf. Eisenhofer and Lechner, *Liturgy of the Roman Rite*, 158-161.

on by wild armies.) There need be no stole for the Deacon, much less a maniple; unless indeed the Deacon do without his dalmatic and leave the tunicle to the Sub-Deacon. Then let him wear the stole. In solemn celebrations which I take it will be the order of every public Mass, there will certainly have to be a Deacon for the Priest, and a Deacon for the congregation. The Deacon of the congregation will not only go round with the plate, but he will also go round with the thurible—incense being a disinfectant.

The object of all my reforms, be it noted, is to remove the entirely superstitious compulsion of forms and ceremonies which have long lost any meaning, and to restore the meaning by destroying the compulsion. For instance, it shall not be necessary for the Priest to read in a buzzing tone at the altar what the Sub-Deacon and Deacon are reading with perfect elocution from their respective lecterns. In the reformed Liturgy we shall never require missals for the laity, since the clergy shall be obliged to make proper use of their own. The Gradual[38] need not be so long-drawn-out, since the people are already comfortably seated, and the Preacher is to go to them instead of them coming to him; or, stay, shall we change all that? Shall we restore the primitive observance in real earnest? There shall be no kneeling at public worship, therefore the holy people of God shall not get in one another's way. Neither shall our churches be cluttered up with pews containing pious libraries and lost rosaries. There will be more room in our churches, and much more encouragement to the people to take an active part, to assist; in plain English to stand around. One of the Popes in the fifth or sixth century complained that he could not hear himself at the altar for the chattering of the young women behind the

---

38 The Gradual is the embellished chant that came after the epistle and before the Gospel in the pre-conciliar form of the Mass. In the post-conciliar Mass its place has been taken by the responsorial psalm.

marble screen. This shows that people stood pretty well round and pretty close to the action of the Mass. I often wonder if the Gradual was prolonged so as to give late comers a chance of hearing the sermon.

ELIMINATIONS, RESTORATIONS, ALTERATIONS

I have said that it is a monstrous thing to expect people to kneel at public worship (it is against all the principles of the Missal even as printed).[39] They are presumed to be standing during all the prayers, and only in penitential seasons is it suggested to them that they should even genuflect, and this is only for the space of one breath, as the Sub-Deacon immediately subjoins "Let us rise up." If the custom of standing at public worship could be revived it would make a great difference to all our manners and customs inside the church. Make your side-chapels as comfortable as you like for private devotion, but the great hall of the church should be as public as a railway station, and as free for traffic; so we should be free to indulge our litanies.[40] I do not mean vehicular traffic.

It is further enacted already in the Missal that there is no kneeling for the whole of Paschal time. One of the most sacred and symbolic things in public worship is that the Priest himself must never kneel. Now for the emergency prayers at the end of Mass the Priest kneels, but who ordered

---

39 From ancient times, and into the Christian period, standing was the normal posture for prayer. Kneeling was the posture of supplication or penitence. By the ninth century kneeling had supplanted standing except in Eastertide, Sundays, and feast days. In John Burchard's rubrics (1502) standing was still the general posture at a sung Mass. cf. Jungmann, *Mass of the Roman Rite* vol. 1, 239-240.

40 Pews are a very late development, and as permanent fixtures in the nave of a church they are a fruit of the Reformation, allowing people to sit for the long sermon which was the focus of Protestant worship.

it?[41] I happen to know at first hand. The first day those prayers were ever said by the Pope himself, the Papal Master of Ceremonies lost his head (as these folk always do when face to face with something fresh). In a kind of hysterical fright he forced the Pope to his knees, the Pope protesting. Some pious authors would see in this an interposition of Divine wisdom. I am not a pious author; I only see in it Italian folly. They have never recovered from the days of Joseph the Second and of Pius the Seventh, who is taking up the whole floor-space of Saint Peter's shrine. He kneels in speechless marble, and —

> His marble soul is in his marble face,
> But he takes up a lot of useful space.

This seems to have been the origin of the pious custom why Popes must kneel. Of course, if every Pope thinks he is the last I should attribute this rather to the Italic temperament, or that which possessed the eighteenth century, cluttering up Westminster Abbey with colossal tombs of schoolmasters and sea-captains, in fact democracy in full bloom. Who shall dare to lay hands upon the Ark?

I would like to preserve all the Latin of the Mass from the end of the catechumens till the Communion. It should not be difficult for the congregation to master the meaning of these beautiful and never-changing prayers; indeed some of them have not changed from the beginning. They are very venerable, among the most venerable things we have after Holy Scripture itself. And yet—and yet, I would eliminate

---

41   The Leonine Prayers, introduced from 1884 under Leo XIII, were added to the end of Mass and were said until 1965. They began as prayers for the defence of the temporal integrity of the Church in the face of growing anti-clericalism and the loss of the papal states. Jungmann considers the priest kneeling for these prayers as "indeed striking." He considers the cause to be the fact that these are the people's prayers, and to embody his solidarity with them in these prayers the priest kneels with them. cf. Jungmann, *Mass of the Roman Rite*, vol. 2, 457.

the new elevation,[42] though it be a thousand years old. It has no business at all at the Consecration. It is all very fine saying that it was introduced as a counter demonstration to the heresies of Berengarius and the wild excesses of Tanchelin.[43]

EXAGGERATIONS

What led up to these excesses, I wonder? May it not be that the real Elevation had been suppressed as a natural consequence of the Priest celebrating with his back to the people? It amounts to this that before Berengarius and Tanchelin drew attention to the fact, the Blessed Sacrament was never seen by the people, and our present expedient of exposition, with the throne mounting higher and higher until it almost touches the roof, is only a lame substitute for the extinction of public worship in this one regard. Even the breaking of the Bread has been eliminated at the Consecration and passes away down to the midst of the prayer for peace, which, after all, does not go further back than the days of Gregory the Great. But, in my estimation, far the most solemn moment of the Liturgy is what is now called the Little Elevation.[44] When I was a small boy this Elevation was so very little that I thought the chalice must be stuck to the altar. This is worth mentioning as a sample of the extraordinary exaggerations developing into abuses, which have always attacked the Liturgy from every side.

Another point is that this is the only moment in our ecclesiastical existence at which the Lord's Prayer is said or

42 Of the host and chalice after each has been consecrated, a practice maintained in the post-conciliar Mass.

43 Berengar of Tours (†1088) and Tanchelm of Antwerp (†1115) both taught against the Real Presence of Christ in the Eucharist. Berengar recanted his heresy and died a Catholic in good standing; Tanchelm died unrepentant at the hand of another priest.

44 At the doxology which concludes the Canon of the Mass, immediately prior to the Lord's Prayer.

sung in the hearing of the many. All the other times it is secret. Why? In the present state of public worship it is more secret than ever in the Canon of the Mass. I should put it where it belongs — the first of all the prayers to be said in public worship before even the Psalm of the Introit. This is not to deny the perfect fitness of its present position.[45]

RESTORATIONS

Along with the true Elevation was suppressed the long triple Prayer for Peace, which begins immediately after the Paternoster and goes right up to the edge of the Communion.[46] It was worse than tantalising during the Great War to have all these solemn prayers as though they were the property of the celebrant alone, thanks to the hullabaloo[47] that wanted things all its own way at that most sacred time. It was worse than tantalising, I repeat, to see that the Pope had, like a good Italian, broken out into eloquent words addressed to the Almighty imploring Peace during the evening service, when this triply solemn petition has remained buried since the seventh century or so.

The Communion of the people follows upon that of the Priest. I cannot help thinking that enormous alterations in these most holy and central things were made for mere convenience. Communion under both kinds could have gone on quite easily if only the office of Deacon had not been to all intents and purposes abolished. Of course, the use of unleavened bread for the Holy Sacrifice makes it almost

---

45 Its present position was established by Pope Gregory the Great. In support of the "perfect fitness" of its present position Jungmann explains its role as the people's prayer to prepare for Communion; cf. *Mass of the Roman Rite,* vol. 2, 278–288.

46 O'Connor is referring to the prayers for peace immediately following the Lord's Prayer, at the commingling of the Host in the Chalice, and immediately following the *Agnus Dei* in the pre-conciliar Mass.

47 i.e., the choir

impossible to use the Greek custom in which the Host is crumbled into the Chalice and then the saturated crumb given. Not that I venerate this as more than an expedient. The theological arguments protecting the change are perfectly valid and compelling, especially as the miracle of Emmaus seems to have been wrought at once for our instruction as to Communion under one kind, though a Belgian Benedictine has taken upon himself (on his own authority) to say that this miracle had no such meaning or intent. The argument from authority is the weakest, but this authority is weaker even than that.

Now, first, as to the form of administration of Holy Communion. The Priest held up the Sacred Elements saying "The Body of our Lord Jesus Christ," and the communicant saying "Amen" immediately received the Holy Eucharist on the centre of his right palm superimposed on the left.[48] Later on, the form of administration became "The Body of our Lord Jesus Christ preserve thee unto life everlasting." This was not pious enough, and so was made into "The Body of our Lord Jesus Christ preserve thy soul unto Life everlasting." (Never use one word where you can get hold of twenty seems to be a principle of some of our pious performers and of others less pious.)

Now when a Priest has to give Communion to as many as five hundred in one morning, the addition of this one word or two would be a most grievous infliction if he had to use the whole of the form for each communicant, especially as he now has to sign the communicant with the sign of the cross.[49] All these are pious insertions put in by those who had nothing to do except be pious. It no more occurred to

---

48 The wording was reduced to "The Body of Christ" with the *Ordo Missae* of 1965, though reception of the host on the hand came later, and then only by dispensation in response to the unapproved reception on the hand that had become common in some countries.

49 This point rather undermines his argument just above that changes to the rite of Communion had been made for "mere convenience."

them what would come afterwards than prophecy occurred to those who builded the tombs of the prophets. I want to point this out with all possible emphasis as an instance of what I mean by the pious fool, a man in whom imbecility takes the form of devotion. There are many such; they are always making us better for worse. One of the tribe in ages long passed into the twilight of fable, discovered that the hand of the communicant was far too profane to touch the Sacred Elements. It did not occur to him that perhaps the tongue was even worse.[50] I may say that it does not seem that any of these things occurred to Jesus Christ Himself (but then He was not pious in the modern sense); but for the pious a cloth had to cover that profane implement called the hand. Of course, the cloth turned out to be of varying grades of whiteness, so a communal cloth was provided. This would at once do away with the Communion under both kinds as practised in the Eastern Church. So the Deacon held the paten under the communicant's chin, and when the Deacon passed away the cloth continued. Now we have a paten of sorts for the very rare possibility of a small particle escaping from the Host. It does this quite often, say once in two hundred times, but I keep seeing priests who purify this paten on principle, whether it needs it or not. This illustrates an accretion in the Liturgy.

Now let us come to the grand accretion of all. There are passionate protests I see in the papers about people leaving

---

50 O'Connor's sarcasm injures his logic. The host received on the hand still has to pass across the tongue. The tradition in the Church developed that only the consecrated hands of a priest, as an *alter Christus*, should touch the Body of Christ. Many would argue that the real point of concern in current practice is not the palm of the hand but the use of the fingers. O'Connor implies a neatly chronological sequence of developments, but Communion on the tongue dates from the ninth century while the Communion cloth appears in the thirteenth century, except for sixth-century Gaul where women had to cover their hands with a cloth. cf. Jungmann, *Mass of the Roman Rite*, vol. 2, 375–381.

church immediately after Mass.[51] I can point out to them that the Celebrant and all concerned left the church immediately after Communion, leaving the sacred vessels to be disposed of by the acolytes. The only prayer after Communion was "On What we have received in the mouth, Lord, may we lay hold with pure minds, and of the temporal gift be to us a remedy for evermore."[52]

Now there is immense waste of time in the ablutions. Another special prayer for the second ablution, and, after much needless delay, another verse of Scripture, and the congregation are once more compelled to attention. Here

---

[51] A case in point, about the time O'Connor has been shown to have been writing, or at least thinking about writing, *Liturgy*: in the letters page of the *Catholic Herald* of 18 February 1938 was a complaint by a priest, "Wales", that communicants "[r]ushing out from Mass just as soon as non-Communicants, lighting cigarettes and gossiping is now the widespread and common behaviour even of otherwise good Catholics. I have tried every way to correct this in my own parish." He further lamented that "Cinemas and wireless have bred a generation of listeners and spectators. When they are not occupied with the use of the eye or the ear they seem thoroughly lost." In reply the following week, "Father of Family" asked parish priests who see "women hurrying out of the church immediately after Mass even though they have been to Holy Communion" if it ever occurred to them that the "majority are mothers or maids who have a heavy morning's work ahead of them," and that for them "Sunday, the family day, is the hardest of the week." He further mused that celibacy might render "clergy blind to the elementary life problems of the housewife." Beneath this letter was another from "An Old Catholic" (sic) lamenting that the "loud talking and laughing ... emptying of money boxes and collection plates; in fact, a general tidying up for at least a quarter of an hour" after Mass make for a "hopeless hindrance to any chance of private prayer after a service."

[52] The prayer has survived in the post-conciliar Mass as the prayer of the priest while purifying the sacred vessels: "What has passed our lips as food, O Lord, may we possess in purity of heart, that what is given to us in time, may be our healing for eternity." O'Connor seems here to have made a later exception into an early rule. A variable prayer of thanksgiving after Communion was common in East and West. However, it seems there was a brief period in which only this prayer was said by the pope after Communion as a public prayer. The evidence is from *Ordo Romanus* IV, which survives only as a fragment and could date from as late as the eleventh century. cf. Jungmann, *Mass of the Roman Rite*, vol. 2, 424–425.

follow Post-Communion prayers. I had seven of them in my first Mass (because I was living in an hysterical state of things). This you would think enough, and the Deacon tells them to go: "Go, 'tis the dismissal," says the Deacon. But do they go? Not a bit of it. There is another prayer to the Blessed Trinity and then the final blessing. You would think that the people would be free to go after this, but I knew a venerable priest (whose will was immensely stronger than his intelligence) make a fearful scene calling back those who had waited for the blessing, that they should wait for the last Gospel as well. Now this business of the last Gospel is getting complicated again. People waited to have the Gospels read for their intention, and it was their pious custom to make it worth the priest's while by a small additional offering. Naturally, the priest would read as many as seven or eight Gospels at their behest, but the others did not wait. When you heard your Gospel read you went away. This was loose without being lax, but those who mistook the one thing for the other, and not before it was time, trimmed all these various Gospels into the Gospel of Saint John which was the favourite among the extras, and is still read for the healing of the sick.[53] (Now we are not finished at the Last Gospel. We have three Hail Mary's (why three?) and the Salve Regina, and a prayer to God our refuge. A year later the prayer to Saint Michael was stuck on, and twenty years later a triple

---

53 The Last Gospel first appears in the thirteenth century in the Dominican Mass, and was not made mandatory in the Roman Rite until 1570. The beginnings of all the gospels were held in high esteem from ancient times, with that of St. John's Gospel preeminent for obvious reasons. Originally the Last Gospel was said by the priest on the way back to the sacristy. The multiplicity of "last gospels" arose from different commemorations coinciding on one day, and so after Mass the priest might say a *Missa sicca* (or sometimes two or three) which comprised only the proper texts for the commemorations not celebrated at the Mass they followed. cf. Jungmann, *Mass of the Roman Rite*, vol. 2, 448–450.

invocation of the Sacred Heart.[54] Is there no end to our unreasonable service?)

Three Hail Marys are now used because one Hail Mary is scarcely a thought, certainly not a word, in Italy. The rule was so far dispensed that the Gospel of that week day (if any) could be read in place of the beginning of Saint John. Now they have altered even that rule, the servants who masquerade as masters, and any special Gospel not read in its proper place in that Mass must be read at the end, as for instance, the Feast of Saint Mary Magdalene occurring on the Sunday. I said servants masquerading as masters because they did not seem to reckon that all the Gospels of the Mass are allowed for in the office of Matins; but under the new regulation they are not allowed for in the Matins, least of all on a Sunday.

I know a famous College, by the way, which never heard of Matins except on the vigil of Christmas (for the Ninth Lesson which is on the Gospel of Saint John all stand up out of special reverence to the Incarnation). Now, on other occasions, I have seen all the students of that College try to make everyone stand during any Ninth Lesson of any Matins. So does ignorance increase and multiply. (Contemporaries please copy.)

I do not class the recitation, even Solemn recitation of the Divine office as public worship. It did not exist at all for many centuries of the Church's early life. It was always optional even on the clergy until Justinian, and can only be called public worship by an extension of the meaning. The only public worship is the Breaking of the Bread. I

---

54 O'Connor is describing the development of the Leonine Prayers mentioned above. Taking the form first decreed by Pius IX as optional prayers at the end of Mass, Leo XIII prescribed three Hail Marys, a *Salve Regina*, a prayer for the conversion of sinners and the liberty of the Church, and the prayer to St. Michael. The triple invocation of the Sacred Heart was added under Pius X.

may instance that in places where they cherish the rules the ordained priests never kneel at the Divine Office. *Never.* This is a formal recognition that the Priest differs in quality from any lesser grade. Besides, the Priest wore vestments of precious texture and flowing pattern, which precluded any such exertions as kneeling. Moreover as he was a Presbyter, that is to say an Elder, his knees were long past that sort of exercise. But hysteria will break up anything, and so the servant masquerading as the master says the Priest must kneel.

The spirit of contradiction is most manifest in the Western custom, universal, that the Priest shall turn his back on the people and at the same time shall turn his back on the altar to say Dominus Vobiscum to the people. Could not this, at least, be done away for a start? It looks and feels absurd, though one absurdity more or less is lost in the crowd.[55]

ALTAR: RESERVATION

The primary motive of these remarks is to burn into the common consciousness that the altar must be in the middle of the place of worship, and it must be an altar and not a repository; cubic, with the table overhanging by four inches all round.[56] (Fortunately these exact measurements do occur

---

55 O'Connor's cavalier attitude on this (for many) touchstone issue evades an interesting liturgical issue arising from it: the mediating role of the celebrant at the altar. "[D]uring the Romanesque Period, it became usual for the priest to say Mass at the opposite side of the altar with his back to the congregation. A contributory factor, and one which paved the way for this change, was the growing tendency for the clergy to be symbolically associated with the congregation in the face of God. In the early days of the Church the priest was the spokesman of God but by the ninth century his role had subtly changed to that of spokesman for his people. Given this new condition it was natural that he should be at the head of the congregation ..." David M. Chappell, "The Development of the Sanctuary and its Furnishings from Early Christian Times to the Present Day" MA Thesis (University of Sheffield, 1963), 96.
56 For Cyril Pocknee this is "the ideal altar," though he does not advocate "imitation nowadays; quite the contrary; that would be make-believe" (Cyril Edward Pocknee, *The Christian Altar in History and Today* [London:

in documents.) At any cost we must rid ourselves of the monstrous accretions before our worship can again be reasonable.

We still have it in the Pontifical that the Blessed Sacrament must not be reserved where High Mass is sung or the Bishop is pontificating. This does away with the Perpetual Solemn Reservation such as we practice in most of our churches. I love to go to the home of the Blessed Sacrament, as most of us do, but I prefer to find it in peace and quietness, and not in the middle of a great hall or a great sanctuary. This is still the custom of the Holy Roman Church, but it is being trampled to pieces all the world over. I see that there were two places of reservation for the Blessed Sacrament in Medieval churches; the hole in the wall was for the reservation from one Mass to another, and the improved "Sacrament House," as still seen in Germany, was for the large Host of Benediction and Procession, and then for those small ones specially kept for the sick. The Sacrament House was invented to obviate the ravages of the damp which attack the Sacred Species in its mural hiding place, but in the Church of Saint Cross in Jerusalem the tabernacle is still to be seen about ten feet up in the wall of the apse, and whether it is used or not it can only be approached by a ladder.[57]

I have not the least desire to go back to the worst customs of late (and early) middle ages, which I think were in themselves an abuse; but in this age of Solemn Reservation, Solemn Procession, Solemn Benediction, Eucharistic Congresses and that, we need a Statute of Limitations. Reservation must *never* be on the High Altar;[58] to permit it, even once, is a

---

A. R. Mowbray, 1963], 22).

57   Up to six means of reserving the Host have been identified: "1) A wall aumbry in the Sacristy. 2) An aumbry in a wall or pillar of the Sanctuary. 3) A tower with a cupboard fashioned in its base. 4) A hanging pyx in the shape of a dove, pelican, cup or palm tree covered with a veil. 5) A movable casket placed on the altar. 6) A tabernacle built into the reredos (very rare)" (Chappell, "Development of the Sanctuary," 26).

58   The reservation of the Blessed Sacrament on the high altar originated in

contradiction of too many important matters, besides which it destroys the real reason for Solemn Processions, which in a pitiful way now go back to where they started, and need never happen all. There used to be a reason for these things and the reason was the transference of the Most Holy from Its secret resting place to the open worship of the High Altar. Anyone who has seen Solemn Benediction in Saint Peter's at Rome will understand the peculiar splendour of this sublime simplicity. The Monstrance is a piece of carved rock crystal not more than ten inches high, and, after being carried round the great church, is deposited on the middle of the great altar. Nothing whatsoever appears on this altar at this moment. There are forests of candles (of which the present writer entirely disapproves), but they are all on the floor; they are not in contact with the altar, and the tremendous small White Host against the dark air space of the nave is better than a wagon drawn by eight milk white steers and in perpetual danger of falling over (as we hear has been done at some of the Eucharistic Congresses). Please, Oh please, let us have a Statute of Limitations—anything to save us from the wild ass—for in Continental churches, and in their base imitations in England, I have been unable to locate the Blessed Sacrament at Exposition because some endeavour had been made to get it right through the roof.

THE CANOPY

The Armenian Rite is older than the Byzantine, and a notable feature of the Armenian Rite is the veil, which, after the Consecration, is agitated above the Sacred Species by deacons standing on each side of the altar. This was originally

---

Rome in the thirteenth century, and spread from there over the next century, influencing the design of the altar "as more and more the altar became subordinated to the tabernacle, and reached a climax in the nineteenth century" (Chappell, "Development of the Sanctuary," 159).

for the good and practical purpose of keeping off the flies. In the Byzantine Rite, from which begins the whole vocabulary of the "awful sacrifice," the "most tremendous sanctuary," and the rest, this almost indispensable fly-flap was altered into a most magnificent tent of brocade all the way from Bagdad, and called "Baldakin" or "Baudequin" from the country of its origin. This presently became a fixture, and now it is a super-tent or an illuminated umbrella in the Roman Basilicas. Indeed it is the blazon of a Basilica. It is sometimes carried in Procession, and I can imagine it borne on the shoulders of four men, to be placed upon the altar as soon as the Offering commences.

The remains of all this are even now seen simplified, crystallised if you will, in the Greek altar, which is still a great cube with a canopy pillared from each of its four corners. So the Baldakin was nailed to the mast.

All this was a huge godsend to that type of devout person who cannot bear anything simple or severe, least of all in Church, so now we tend to have what we call a "Baldacchino" (really a canopy or a pent-roof) and to call it a Baldacchino is like calling a week-end cottage an umbrella, or vice-versa.[59] The canopy in due course became a kind of hat-rack for all manner of pendant crosses, lamps, and gold crowns. In the Greek Church the pyx is suspended over the altar in the form of a dove. All this superfluous wealth grew so that an attic had to be practised in the canopy to contain all the treasures. When the pyx was reserved in this ciborium veils were hung about, even as they had been hung about the altar in the

---

59 The description here is ambiguous. There are two types of altar canopy: the stone ciborium, resting on four stone columns, which covers the entire area of the altar including the area where the celebrant stands; and the textile or wood baldachin (or tester), suspended from the ceiling or back wall. The ciborium is the older form. In O'Connor's day a canopy was required for any altar on which the Blessed Sacrament was reserved, and for a cathedral's high altar. It serves to give honour and focus to the altar. cf. O'Shea, *Worship of the Church*, 172–173; and Pocknee, *Christian Altar*, 55–59.

Byzantine Rite. In the period of Holy Terror, the veil and the barrier joined hands and became the iconostasis (mark that neither of them had any justification in tradition); but the iconostasis to this day forms a perfect barrier between the Celebrant and the congregation, though yet it has not ruined public worship like our still more illustrious rood-screens. Here is a catalogue of monstrous innovations which are now venerable relics. The one thing common to them all is that they are entirely anonymous and wholly without sanction. *Note* that in poor churches instead of gorgeous brocade, linen was permitted, and, this being cheap, could flow down all round the altar; and this is the grandmother of our altar cloths which are prescribed to touch the ground.

The ciborium proper or tabernacle above the baldacchino is only a twelfth century innovation, conspicuously absent from the older canopies.

THE ALTAR I[60]

When the decorated shrine by the local genius ran from East to West behind the altar it resembled our present-day altars with the tabernacle in the middle, but the local genius was not satisfied; the shrine had to run from North to South to show its magnificence, and the altar did not look so well underneath the top-heavy bulk. Then developments began in opposite directions. The altar was made wider than the shrine for purely aesthetic considerations, and the cube disappeared from that day to this.[61]

---

60 This section finds general agreement in O'Shea, *Worship of the Church,* pp.167–171. O'Connor must surely have read Edmund Bishop's account of the altar's development, with which his own aligns. cf. Bishop, "The Christian Altar," in *Liturgica Historica,* 20–38, especially 25ff. However, Pocknee directly repudiates Bishop's thesis, "as copied by a number of commentators," that the advent of reliquaries was the cause of the celebrant to cease facing the people, holding it "will no longer bear serious investigation." *Christian Altar,* 93–94.
61 cf. Chappell, "Development of the Sanctuary," 111.

The next development was — the gorgeous shrine was bodily moved back to the end of the apse; and the altar once again was free. A fool's a fool for all that, and the reredos was invented to take the place of the shrine for fear, by any chance, the priest might once more face the congregation in celebrating the Sacred Mysteries, so the altar became permanently a sideboard.[62] The ruthlessness of insane convention is nowhere better seen than in such instances as the glorious High Altar of Assisi (great and simple like the High Altar at Saint Peter's), but for centuries burdened with a superstructure like a cathedral organ; or again in the Church of Saints Cosmas and Damian, where one of the most famous mosaics in the whole world is obliterated by a wooden kind of hen-roost, intended, of course, to enhance the importance of the holy altar. Some of these reredoses are magnificent works of invention and even of suggestion, but you have to peer at them to find the altar. Naturally, not everyone could afford one of these, so that sublime creation called the Altar-piece was devised by the willing painter. The altar was back against the wall everywhere — both the high altar and the bye altar were back against the wall for the sake of the Altar-piece — and the super-altar or retable was invented to be a pedestal for the sublime miracle of the brush. The present writer has seen the retable enlarged to three storeys in order to hold candles in bottles, and field flowers in coffee canisters for really great occasions.

When con-celebration died it was enacted somehow that no one but the Pope in Rome could celebrate on a High Altar. As the Pope was frequently not in Rome at all (or was still more frequently prevented from celebrating), on great days, for the comfort of the holy people of God the High Altar was covered with all the treasures of the Church, reminding

---

62   Ninian Comper also used "sideboard" to describe this sort of altar: Ninian Comper, *Of the Christian Altar and the Buildings Which Contain It* (London: Society for Promoting Christian Knowledge, 1950), 56.

one of the best repository windows; or, as someone put it once, "A street fight in heaven."[63] I wonder if this wholesale destruction of churches and the transmigration of jewelled reliquaries to Jewish drawing-rooms[64] is divinely intended to wean us off these venerable and ruinous customs, for, mark you, the upshot of them all is that the altar scarcely exists except as a decoration at one end of the church. Apart from the question "Which side was right at the Reformation"—a question which long ago settled itself—we have to reckon on the damage done to the whole Christian mentality by infinite Bible-chopping and by making theology synonymous with contradiction. At least it had issue in our Art; stateliness perished for the sake of convenience, and convenience itself became unwieldy with Baroque creations, for religion ceased to be contemplative and tried to be all demonstrative, if only by exaggerating what the other side hated. It was great fun when the other side began to copy all this, as in Saint Paul's in London.

Have we said enough to show that stunning the average man is a poor substitute for the deep meaning of public worship? Stunning him through his eye or through his ear, it matters little which. He is equally driven away from contact with the Divine. Father forgive them—they know not what

---

63   This practice, of Gallican origin, dates from the ninth century, with a pastoral letter by Hincmar of Rheims (or possibly Pope Leo IV); an "innovation that was to have considerable effect in the construction and development of the altar" and "an invasion of a principle which, until then, had been carefully observed" (Pocknee, *Christian Altar*, 84). The advent of reliquaries on the altar led to the development of gradines, or shelves, behind the altar in the tenth century on which to place the growing number of reliquaries and fostering the change of the celebrant's position at the altar. cf. Chappell, "Development of the Sanctuary," 96.

64   This casual jibe is more reflective of a lazy and unfiltered expression of contemporary social attitudes than any anti-Semitic conviction on O'Connor's part. It is clearly being used for rhetorical effect, and it should be noted that given the private circulation of this tract, it is rhetoric he seems never to have employed in public.

they do; but when their ignorance makes them vain — My God, why hast Thou forsaken us?

It would be very interesting and instructive to found a Society, self-supporting of course, for the perfect rationalising of the church and the altar, the vesture and the ceremonial, because to get rid of the trappings and the trimmings would require a great deal of time and discreet trying on and trying out; indeed, since all these overwhelming and overlapping abuses came in through a lack of consciousness, they can only be got rid of by constant and conscious effort.

When the altar was enlarged beyond the dreams of avarice it craved something to conceal the aching void. The earliest medieval altar furniture consisted of the cross on one side and one candle on the other.[65] The aesthetic sense could not stand that; the cross was put in the centre with a candle on each side. This was semi-permanent for Low Mass let us say. For High Mass came another cross and two more candles, and these were brought round to face the Celebrant at the Sanctus — hence four candles at Solemn Celebration; but we have documentary evidence that Innocent III had only two, even on great days.[66] We are blandly assured that seven candles is the correct number when the Bishop sings High Mass (this because it was the Roman custom to have seven candles carried in procession by seven Sub-Deacons of the seven Regions of Rome).[67] There is no evidence for this until the 13th century, and then we begin a hideous altercation as to

---

65 The reference is to the supposition that the altar cross derives from the processional cross that was placed beside the altar on arrival, and later detached from its shaft and placed on the altar itself. cf. Eisenhofer and Lechner, *Liturgy of the Roman Rite*, 129.

66 cf. Bishop, *Liturgica Historica*, 311.

67 Indeed, the consensus endured that this papal procession is the origin of any candles near the altar at Mass. cf. O'Shea, *Worship of the Church*, 176; Eisenhofer and Lechner, *Liturgy of the Roman Rite*, 129. Pocknee notes that setting the number of candles on the altar to six (or seven for pontifical Masses) occurred as late as the seventeenth century; *Christian Altar*, 41.

whether the candles were to be put on the altar or on the floor. They could not be put on the altar unless it was of ample dimensions.[68] There is monumental evidence going back to the ninth century that from the canopy or ciborium depended seven lamps, not candles but oil lamps, for the Pontifical celebration. The seven lamps were always a sacred institution from the great temple onwards, typifying the seven spirits who stand before the throne, but the Popes in the middle ages were very seldom free to indulge their symbolic proclivities. They often had to say Mass where they could, and the seven lamps were as much a pious aspiration as a reality. When the seven candlesticks could be carried by the seven Sub-Deacons well and good. They had more often to do without, though we have it that five candles were carried during the singing of the Latin Gospel, and two for the Greek.[69]

This is a very interesting illustration of the gentle pressure between wanting a thing and being able to afford it. When time and place and circumstances afforded it the seven candles were in use, but much more often were there only two, and these were not upon the altar, but on the floor. There is no justification for the ugly six in a row which do so much damage to mere appearance on our altars, and the seven, being the seven Regions, etc., smack suspiciously of Durandus and his absurd symbolic interpretations of everything.

To have the Crucifix upon the altar for Mass is a grave contravention of the great rubric and tradition of the Roman Church, which bars all emblems of the Passion from the Real Presence. The theology of this should be obvious even

---

68 Candles are accepted as having been put on the altar by the eleventh century, and for some this appears to be connected to the growing movement of altars up against walls. Chappell argues it may have begun in Gaul as early as the eighth or ninth century. cf. O'Shea, *Worship of the Church*, pp.176–177; Eisenhofer and Lechner, *Liturgy of the Roman Rite*, 129; Chappell, "Development of the Sanctuary," 127–128.

69 cf. Bishop, *Liturgica Historica*, 306.

to the very devout. It is a reminder that the Eucharist precedes Calvary in point of time and even of importance, and follows it up for ever, so that Calvary is an episode of the Eucharist and is *inside* the Institution. This is the Priesthood according to the order of Melchisedeck. But we got to thinking that without a Crucifix on the altar the Consecration would somehow not be valid.[70] Such is the power of crass ignorance that we have would-be affecting pictures of a priest raising the chalice towards a shadowy crucifixion.[71]

These liberties with strict theology are very dangerous, and have even led to heresy in the past. We are far from despising the Crucifix as an object of devotion or even a piece of altar-furniture, though we are quite prepared to be shown that its place is never on the altar during Mass any more than during Exposition. But what shall we say of the Altar Cards and of the Missal? They began as a necessary evil due to the infirmities of the clerical memory, much resembling that of others, but it is no uncommon thing to find the most fantastic rococo metal frames encumbering an altar — metal frames weighing several stone — and the text entirely illegible, being microscopically condensed to allow play to the gorgeous frame. If this is not palpably absurd, what is?

---

70 A permanent plain cross on the altar can be traced with certainty only to the late twelfth century. Very often it was removed after Mass. Up to about the ninth century placing anything on the altar other than cloths, chalice, and paten, and the Mass and Gospel books was not allowed. The crucifix on the altar was mandated from 1746. cf. O'Shea, *Worship of the Church*, 174f; and Gregory Dix, *The Shape of the Liturgy* (Westminster: Dacre Press, 1945), 412; Pocknee, *Christian Altar*, 41, 84.

71 The first altar crucifixes depicted Christ's triumph rather than His passion, with the corpus upright, vested and crowned. "During the thirteenth century the crown of glory over the image of Christ was changed to a crown of thorns and it encircled the head of the figure, bent earthwards. Therefore, not only did the crucifix become a permanent ornament of the altar but the purpose of the cross changed from a symbol of the majesty of Christ triumphing over death, to a reminder of the sufferings Christ underwent to atone for sin." Chappell, "Development of the Sanctuary," 127.

The Holy Gospels alone were allowed to rest upon the altar in the primitive observance. Of this we still have a trace when the Deacon lays the Gospels on the altar while he prays for inspiration and vocal powers. The Lectionary was never on the altar — only the Book of the Gospels. The Proper of the Mass was ministered by varying ministers from varying manuscripts, and the Canon would be ministered by a Sub-Deacon facing the Celebrant across the altar.[72] Arrangement and accommodation are needed at Low Mass if no server be available. Now a Low Mass presumes the absence of a server! Strictly speaking, it never really happened, but with the cessation of con-celebration came in Low Mass, very properly introduced under monastic auspices, lest the abbot be mistaken for a bishop. So the ministers, growing more and more hopelessly incompetent, could not be expected to hold the book in the right position for the Celebrant, and it was laid on a cushion on the altar while the minister went to see to other things, as Saint Philip's lay-brother used to tidy up his room while he was in ecstasy at the altar.

The present writer would also like to do away completely with the habit of shifting the book from one side to the other. The Missal could be printed in sections as it was in the beginning; The Lectionary, the Book of the Gospels and the Sacramentary with Prefaces, Canon and Collects, or the Book of the Celebrant, the Book of the Deacon and the Book of the Sub-Deacon. To minster these various books at Low Mass would give the server something to do and keep

---

72   The texts of the Mass were collected according to the person using them: celebrant, deacon, sub-deacon, and cantors. The celebrant's particular texts were gathered in *libelli* which were suited to the liturgical occasion. These came to be gathered into sacramentaries. The missal properly speaking, the *missale plenum*, which gathered in it all the texts for the celebration of Mass for use at Low or private Masses, developed between the eighth and tenth centuries. cf. Adrian Fortescue, *The Mass: A Study of the Roman Liturgy* 3rd Edition (London: Longmans, Green & Co, 1937), 113ff, 189-190; O'Shea, *Worship of the Church*, 48; Eisenhofer and Lechner, *Liturgy of the Roman Rite*, 26-27.

him from examining the congregation too narrowly. It has fallen to my lot to be implored over a period of months, at any cost to get rid of a certain "monkey" who seemed to be possessed at the altar.

Note well that I would not sweep away wholesale, but would suit my ceremonial to my circumstances. It is the paralysis of this faculty which has led us into the mire.

I would like to point out that the major reform is to restore the altar to its proper position in the Church, and to its proper use, which is the celebration of the Eucharist and the Solemn Exposition of the same; then all else will grow naturally to its proper place and size.

THE PLACE OF WORSHIP

A large room in a private house was evidently, from the Gospel, the first place of worship. I am inclined to think that it was smaller and cosier than the outer hall with its fireplace, in which they slew and roasted the Paschal Lamb, and ate it with their loins girded and with staves in their hands in honour of the great journey through the desert.

When this was ended and the remains of the lamb burned on the fire, the little company adjourned to the inner room, great and ready spread for the feast of great rejoicing in honour of the arrival at the Promised Land. This was more commonly observed in Jerusalem and district as an addition to the Paschal Feast, and here history begins, for it was on their reclining at this inner table that our Lord went round and washed their feet in token of welcome. Sweet compotes of fruit and finer bread, and sweet white wine, were the special properties of this light thanksgiving feast, hence the discrepancy between East and West about leavened and unleavened bread.

It was the first day of the Azymes, and, unleavened bread being used with the Paschal Lamb, it would be natural for the

Apostolic tradition from Galilee to remember the unleavened bread in the after recurrence of the Eucharistic Feast, but the people of the Capital, having more resource of service, would be able to utilise a fine and leavened bread for the Eucharist. Hence Jerusalem with Saint James kept its ancient custom, while the countryside adopted the unleavened bread. This is my own speculation on the standing great discrepancy on such a matter as this between the Eastern Church and the Western.[73] Both have always been agreed that white wine was to be used because white wine was often sweeter and more expensively prepared than red. Red wine may have been in common use with the meat. I think that our Lord's words "I will not drink of this fruit of the vine until I drink it new with you in the Kingdom" were His solemn toast to the end of the Old Law, drunk over the Paschal Lamb. The New Wine of the Kingdom I conjecture to be the white wine of the Eucharist.[74] We have chapter and verse for this, since an heresiarch of the early third century, who gave himself out as the incarnation of the Holy Spirit (hitherto rather neglected), gave as his credentials his power of effecting transubstantiation in the chalice, that is to say, he changed the

---

73   In St. John's Gospel, the Last Supper is not identified as a Passover meal, whereas in the synoptic gospels it is. In the Passover meal, the Jews use only unleavened bread, symbolic of the haste with which they fled Egypt, with no time to finish preparing the bread as normal. Moreover, leaven or yeast in the New Testament often represents hypocrisy (eg. Matt 16:6, Luke 12:1) or sin (1 Cor 5:6–8). However, most eastern churches use leavened bread as they look beyond the Last Supper's Passover context to the resurrection of Christ and the heavenly banquet, for which they hold the completeness of leavened bread to be more appropriate. cf. Jungmann, *Mass of the Roman Rite,* vol. 2, 31ff.
74   The Church has never legislated on the colour of sacramental wine. Red may seem a more fitting colour for signifying the Real Presence of Christ in the Precious Blood of the chalice, yet white or amber wine accords more with the Catholic teaching that the Mass is an unbloody memorial of the sacrifice of the Cross. More prosaically it may be that red wine fell out of favour due to its tendency to stain altar linen. Contradicting O'Connor, Jungmann holds that red wine was preferred in the East (*Mass of the Roman Rite,* vol. 2, 37).

white wine into red at the consecration. He was discovered to have a bladder of red wine up his sleeve, and so he faded away; but his adventure is valuable as a sidelight on the practice of the early Church, East and West.

Jerusalem was specially privileged to immolate the Paschal Lamb after sunset on Thursday, as then the Parasceve began, because of the enormous number of immolations at home and in the temple which were taking place on the great day itself. Hence we justify our supposition that the Paschal Lamb was slain by our Lord with His disciples at sunset on the Thursday.

THE ALTAR II

There is no doubt at all in tradition that the first altar used by our Lord Himself, and afterwards by Saint Peter, was a shallow chest with a small drawer for such things as the knife and the linen cloth. The bread, before breaking, would be scored by the knife. This chest is very authentically preserved to the present hour in Saint John Lateran, and the tradition of a wooden altar was so strong that even now in the Greek Church stone altars must have some wood. But we Westerns have changed all that, and in Saint Prisca there is a marble slab with an eleventh century inscription to the effect that it was upon this table that Saint Peter celebrated the Sacred Mysteries. There is not necessarily any misreading of tradition in this, for Saint Peter could plant his portable altar on a marble table such as was very common in Rome, but, broadly speaking, any table would suffice for celebration in the early days. In the catacombs it is a tripod, and the priest stands facing the female figure praying with uplifted arms and typifying the whole Church. The question of the arcosolium[75] need not detain us, because half a dozen

---

75   The arched niche or recess for a tomb in the catacombs.

bystanders would dreadfully incommode any celebrant at an arcosolium, so that this celebration could hardly be classed as public worship. The same applies to celebration on the flat top of a sarcophagus containing the body of a martyr.[76]

For public worship the table would be set in the middle, or as near as possible to the middle, of the best room in the house. This is plain to see in the basilicas; even ruined basilicas which never had Mass said in them at any time can still show their white marble bar across the top step leading to the judgment-seat in the apse. Misreading and misapplication of this bar led to the first sanctuary-rails, but the altar was put on the very edge of the top step in the earliest adapted basilicas, because that was as nearly central as might be fitting. We must not imagine large congregations in the primitive Church; there were various reasons against such, and the celebrant stood at a central table facing his congregation, just as the host with his guests.

The tribune behind the altar was naturally the seat of the Bishop and his clergy con-celebrating, just as the Senatorial court-room so lodged in the same place the Judge and his Assessors. The Papal High Mass contains quite picturesque reminders of this progress between the altar and the throne. It is one of the few really enlightening monuments we have about primitive usage, but what I wish to emphasise here is that the only usage for a thousand years was a central altar with the celebrant on one side and the people on the other. There was no barrier, for that had ceased to exist with the old basilica; not even the steps were retained, save perhaps one, and at Sant'Apollinare in Classe there still stands a fifth century altar, very central and without any decoration, and only large enough for one man to celebrate and handle the Sacred Elements. There is no room for books or candles or

---

76   Jungmann likewise dismisses the idea of regular public Masses in the catacombs (*Early Liturgy*, 14–15).

crucifixes, or trimmings of any kind, for one of the oldest rubrics was that the altar should harbour nothing but the materials for the Eucharist Itself. Even they were not put on until the business part of the Mass, and the Sub-Deacon now holds the paten at High Mass at the foot of the altar to keep all unconsecrated offerings from the holy table. Another most ancient and stringent rubric is that there must be no emblems of the Passion where the Eucharist is in action, i.e., no competition. Figure to yourself how two thousand years of forgetfulness, misunderstanding, foreign invasion and ignorance and indolence would eat into all these observances. To kiss the Bishop's ring before receiving from him is a gross contravention of true reverence, French in origin. Then imagine the enormous and loud-mouthed tribe of servants masquerading as masters, or the misinformed educating the misbegotten, and you will have some idea of how these quite clear and simple things became mixed and impossible to handle. Nobody now dreams of keeping any of them, but the confusions very much hinder public worship.

The solemn altar most favoured by the pagans was a very beautiful thing — a seamless round block of marble, nearly breast high, carved round with figures in high relief — and may still be seen (possibly on its original site) in the Villa Pamphili. To copy such a thing as this would have been an abomination in Rome up to about the seventh century, but the High Altar (as distinct from the bye altar) became a cubic block of three foot dimension typifying the worship which shall not pass away.

So universal was the custom of central altars that even side altars in great churches were constructed as pulpits so that the priest must needs face outwards. The idea of the priest turning his back to the people and getting between them and the great deed would certainly have caused a sensation in the first thousand years, but mark how brutal innovations altered all this. First, the relics of the saints were under the altar, as Scripture takes for granted. In the ninth century the savage Lombards raided the tombs of the martyrs in such wholesale fashion that Saint Pascal the Second spent days carting the sacred remains inside the city walls, and countless thousands now are resting in the Pantheon or Church of All Saints. He it was that took Saint Cecily's body from her tomb in her crypt and laid it under the altar in her own house. Meanwhile the rude and ruthless Lombards had got away with a deal of plunder, and rich Benedictine abbots were quite rightly offering hospitality in their Abbey churches to these sacred remains. It was an ambition with every abbot to have a martyr under his high altar. It was also an ambition of the wealthy Abbey to "build the tombs of the prophets" with all the wealth of design and colour that could be afforded locally, but the more gorgeous the shrine the greater the chagrin that it should be lost from view. It was, therefore, raised above the altar, and now the priest, through reverence for a dead body, turns his back on the Mystic Body and begins to worship face to the wall. Note how ill weeds grow. The gorgeous shrine would be placed end on, above the altar, but the artist would still be peeved, and to please him they would put the shrine lengthwise, when it was found to make the altar look absurd and top heavy, so for purely aesthetic reasons the altar was widened until it was in some churches now the length of a Sabbath day's journey. It also had to contain candles to illustrate the shrine. The shrine got more and more gorgeous; the altar went wider and wider, until now we have those famous Flemish dorsals regardless of expense, which are almost too wide for the whole sanctuary, and are often closed on week-days like museums and such places. Even Pugin did not appear to go so far as this. He often designed very beautiful altars and sanctuaries; for instance, in Maynooth in the middle of an arcaded apse he set the high altar, a stately and simple thing, but your average sensual man with more money than brains left three thousand pounds in his will for something that the ignorant should call beautiful, a forest of white marble pinnacles which obliterate the whole grace of a very graceful building, and would be much improved by any judicious iconoclast. But whatever is done now, the priest must face the wall. Decorate the wall as much as you like and call it a reredos — it is still a back wall and the high altar is only a side-board. The absurdity of all this comes out on special occasions, as, for instance, at the consecration of a Bishop, when there is nowhere for the consecrated Bishop to stand in order to con-celebrate in due form with his Consecrator, nowhere but the Epistle side of the altar. If the altar were as Christians intended, he would stand facing his Consecrator on the other side of the altar. Then on the consecration of the altar itself, the simple-minded rubric lays down that the Thurifer shall go round and round the altar incensing while the consecration ceremony is being completed. Instead of this, in the majority of cases, the unfortunate Thurifer has to walk to and fro behind all the ministers "wasting his sweetness on the desert air."[77]

What we wish to point out by these remarks is the extraordinary infamy of these accretions of the ages, and the end was not yet when the altar was made absurd. The great city churches, when roofed, were used as exchanges and covered markets (especially in bad weather) for the whole town. Paul's Churchyard was really Paul's Church, the biggest nave in Christendom. What authority have we for uttering these profanities? It is written in the life of Saint Charles Borromeo that at the very end of the 16th century, two generations after Martin Luther, he sealed up the far door of Milan Cathedral just to stop the local custom of driving laden donkeys and mules across the great nave at all hours, as a short cut to the vegetable market. Even now I read in a serious work that

---

77   From Thomas Gray "Elegy Written in a Country Churchyard" (1751).

pelota is played in the nave of the Cathedral of Auxerre;[78] hence the massive rood-screen in so many of the churches, together with the almost equally massive choir-screen running the whole circuit of the apse, as in Chartres, York Minster, and other places. The rood-screen was made the thickness of a house because of the rough stuff which went on in the nave, and whereas the altar may have been facing down the church it now had to be pushed back against the end wall to get it further away from the thunder of the cattle and the shouting of the merchants. Your cathedral choir is a church within a church, but we spend millions in base imitation of what ought never to have been allowed, and we still elaborate arguments about the use of the rood-screen. It is only useful where the congregation are mostly cattle. I trust this is not the ambition of any restorer of the Liturgy.

Cockle has been oversown whilst men were sleeping. They must sleep sometimes. They must also wake sometimes and not deny too indignantly that they were sleeping. We simply cannot afford to waste our churches, our chances, and our time in Church, looking on at people doing something we are not clear about, singing or saying what we do not understand. Latin is lovely to say or sing, but its usefulness is less than its decorative value. Its imperative unalterable prescriptive rights are now changed into wrongs. They are the fossilised Imperialism of the world's great capital City, to use the least abusive epithet. Latin is in fact the monument to the vernacular in public worship, for it was the vernacular of Europe before Europe had any written languages. Stop writing to the papers and begin to think.

---

78 Certainly, from circa 1396 to 1538, the canons of Auxerre cathedral would gather around its labyrinth on Easter Sunday to play a ball game considered by some to be a liturgical dance, using a leather ball thrown between the canons while they danced and sang the Easter sequence, *Victimae paschali laudes*. cf. Max Harris, *Sacred Folly: A New History of the Feast of Fools* (Ithaca: Cornell University Press, 2011), 56–60.

If the Kingdom of Heaven suffer violence it can also suffer degeneration, whilst men are sleeping. To forget the reason of a sacred rite and go on with it when it has ceased to be reasonable is degeneracy, but still more is it degenerate to omit stately ways of implementing what is of precept. Idolatry goes on after the idol is proven dead. Candles should be used for illumination, now they are used for conflagration, or the playthings of a brainless sacristan.

Language is a manifestation of thought, music is its decoration. Music must not destroy the thought or the feeling; it is intended to publish the sense more thoroughly to heart and brain. But oh! what a sorry noise it is become! The vocal defectives drag down the rest, and even choirmasters are slow to spot those voices which make silence lovelier than any music. Whole choirs can and do degenerate to such a pass as this, whilst the priest at the altar consoles himself by thanking God he is not being sensual, forgetting that he is being senseless. Congregations ruin rhythm, which depends on drill. Drill is a mechanical device to ensure that the given herd will obey promptly. No herd will do this spontaneously, and even the organist will play up and down to the slackers, thinking he is being charitable or tolerant or something. The price of Public Worship that is worshipful is eternal vigilance.

APHORISMS

1. Truth is refreshing, even if it blow through a broken window.

2. Draughts may be fatal to those who live the sheltered life.

3. Piety is only one of the Seven Gifts of the Holy Ghost. Wisdom and Understanding be two more. Yet there be those who try to make Piety serve for all.

(For private circulation only.)

ABOUT THE EDITOR

Dom Hugh Somerville Knapman is a Benedictine monk and priest of Douai Abbey near Reading, England. He is the author of *Ecumenism of Blood: Heavenly Hope for Earthly Communion* (Paulist Press, 2018) and the editor of *A Limerickal Commentary on the Second Vatican Council* (Arouca Press, 2020). Currently he is pursuing doctoral studies at St Mary's University, Twickenham.